Climate Change and Small Islands: Strengthening Water Security by Building Resilience, Managing Demand, Upgrading Infrastructure, Protecting Quality, and Financing Adaptation

Copyright

Climate Change and Small Islands: Strengthening Water Security by Building Resilience, Managing Demand, Upgrading Infrastructure, Protecting Quality, and Financing Adaptation

ISBN (eBook): 978-1-991370-90-7

ISBN (Paperback): 978-1-991370-91-4

Published by Our Future Water

First Edition, 2025

Cover design and interior layout by Our Future Water

Table of Contents

Introduction

Small islands stand at the forefront of climate vulnerability, facing distinctive challenges in securing reliable and sustainable water resources.

The Vulnerability of Small Islands

Small islands are inherently vulnerable due to their geographic isolation, small land area, and limited freshwater resources. Surrounded by vast expanses of ocean, these islands often depend on rainfall and shallow groundwater lenses to meet their water needs, leaving them highly susceptible to climatic variability. Their low elevation makes them particularly prone to sea level rise, coastal erosion, and saltwater intrusion, which threaten both water quality and quantity. Economic limitations and constrained institutional capacity further amplify their sensitivity to external shocks, while population growth and increasing tourism can strain already limited supplies. The combination of physical, environmental, and socioeconomic factors places small islands among the world's most at-risk regions when it comes to water security in a changing climate.

Why Focus on Small Islands Now?

Small islands are on the front lines of climate change, experiencing its impacts earlier and more intensely than many other regions. Rising sea levels are already leading to the inundation of coastal areas and the contamination of freshwater sources with saltwater, while shifts in rainfall patterns bring both severe droughts and intense storms that challenge water management systems. These islands often lack the scale and financial resources needed for large-scale infrastructure projects, making adaptation particularly urgent and complex. At the same time, their unique circumstances and innovative responses can provide valuable lessons for larger nations confronting similar threats in the future. The combination of immediate risk and potential for global learning makes the water security and climate resilience of small islands a critical topic. Addressing their needs not only supports the survival and well-being of island communities but also advances international goals for climate adaptation and sustainable development.

Purpose and Structure of the Book

This book aims to provide a comprehensive overview of the strategies available to enhance water security and build climate resilience on small islands. Recognizing the diversity and complexity of these environments, the text is organized into nine chapters that systematically address the challenges and opportunities unique to island contexts. Following this introduction, the chapters examine the broad climate threats faced by small islands, the characteristics of their water resources, and the principles of integrated water resources management tailored for these settings. Subsequent sections explore climate-resilient infrastructure, demand management, water quality protection, policy and governance frameworks, and the vital role of community engagement. A dedicated chapter focuses on the specific financing needs and solutions for water security and adaptation. The book concludes by summarizing key insights and presenting actionable recommendations. Throughout, the aim is to offer practical guidance grounded in the realities of small island settings, supporting policymakers, practitioners, and community leaders as they navigate an increasingly uncertain future.

Chapter 1: The Climate Change Challenge for Small Islands

Small islands are among the most vulnerable regions to the impacts of climate change, facing an array of interconnected challenges that threaten their water security, livelihoods, and long-term sustainability. Their geographic isolation, limited land area, and dependence on climate-sensitive resources make them especially sensitive to rising sea levels, shifting rainfall patterns, and the increasing frequency of extreme weather events. These pressures are compounded by social, economic, and infrastructural constraints, leaving many island communities with little margin for error. As climate change accelerates, the risks to freshwater availability, ecosystem health, and economic stability intensify, demanding urgent and innovative responses. This chapter examines the unique characteristics of small islands, explores the specific climate threats they face, and sets the stage for understanding the urgency of building resilience. By identifying the drivers and consequences of climate vulnerability, we lay the groundwork for effective adaptation and water security strategies.

1.1 Unique Geophysical and Socioeconomic Features

Small islands are defined by a set of unique geophysical and socioeconomic characteristics that shape their vulnerability and resilience to climate change and water security challenges.

Geographically, small islands are typically isolated land masses surrounded by ocean, often located far from major continents and frequently clustered in archipelagos. Their land area is limited, which constrains the extent of terrestrial resources available for human use, agriculture, and water storage. Many small islands are low-lying, with coastlines exposed to tidal surges, sea level rise, and extreme weather events. The geology of these islands often results in shallow, fragile groundwater systems such as freshwater lenses, which are easily affected by over-extraction and saltwater intrusion. In addition, rainfall is often highly seasonal and variable, leading to periods of both water scarcity and excess that can be difficult to manage with limited infrastructure.

Socioeconomically, small island populations are diverse, ranging from densely populated urban centers to sparsely inhabited rural communities. Many island economies are heavily dependent on a narrow range of sectors, such as tourism, fisheries, and agriculture, which are themselves vulnerable to environmental and climate shocks. The small size of these economies can result in limited access to financial resources, technology, and skilled labor, further constraining the capacity for investment in water infrastructure and adaptation measures. Social structures in small islands often reflect strong community ties and cultural traditions, which can support collective action but may also create challenges in integrating new practices and technologies.

The interplay between geographic isolation, limited natural resources, and socioeconomic constraints creates a context where water security and climate resilience are especially complex. Understanding these unique features is critical to developing strategies that are both effective and appropriate for the realities faced by small island communities.

1.2 Climate Change Threats

Climate change presents a multitude of interconnected threats to small islands, making them some of the most exposed and least resilient environments in the world. The impacts of global warming are particularly pronounced for these territories due to their small size, low elevation, and dependence on climate-sensitive resources. The consequences are already visible in many regions, affecting ecosystems, infrastructure, livelihoods, and—crucially—water security.

One of the most significant threats is sea level rise. As global temperatures increase, glaciers and polar ice sheets are melting and oceans are expanding, resulting in higher sea levels. For small islands, even modest increases can lead to the inundation of coastal zones, erosion of beaches, and the submergence of low-lying areas. This not only reduces available land but also contaminates freshwater lenses with saltwater, making it increasingly difficult to access safe drinking water. Coastal infrastructure, such as ports, roads, and water supply systems, faces heightened risks from both gradual and sudden changes, including tidal flooding and storm surges.

Changes in precipitation patterns pose another critical challenge. Climate change is altering the frequency, intensity, and distribution of rainfall across many island regions. Some islands are experiencing more frequent and severe droughts, leading to reduced surface water flows and lower groundwater recharge. Others are subject to heavier rainfall events that can overwhelm existing drainage systems, cause flooding, and increase sediment and contaminant runoff into water supplies. The variability and unpredictability of rainfall complicate planning for water storage and allocation, forcing communities to adapt quickly to changing conditions.

Rising temperatures also bring direct and indirect risks. Warmer air and sea surface temperatures contribute to higher evaporation rates, intensifying water loss from soil, reservoirs, and vegetation. Elevated temperatures can also increase the demand for water in agriculture, industry, and households, placing further stress on already limited resources. In marine environments, warming waters threaten coral reefs and fisheries that many island economies depend on, while also disrupting the delicate balance of coastal ecosystems.

The frequency and intensity of extreme weather events—such as tropical cyclones, hurricanes, and typhoons—are expected to increase with climate change. These events bring destructive winds, heavy rains, and storm surges that can devastate infrastructure, uproot communities, and disrupt water and sanitation systems. Recovery from such events is often slow and costly, particularly for small islands with limited resources and capacity.

Finally, climate change interacts with existing environmental pressures, amplifying their effects. For example, over-extraction of groundwater can make freshwater lenses more susceptible to saltwater intrusion, while land use changes can increase runoff and pollution during storms. The cumulative impact of these stressors makes water management more challenging and raises the stakes for effective adaptation.

Taken together, these climate change threats are reshaping the physical, economic, and social landscapes of small islands. Addressing them requires a deep understanding of local conditions, proactive planning, and the implementation of strategies that build both immediate resilience and long-term sustainability for island water systems and communities.

1.3 Water Resource Pressures

Small islands face a unique and complex set of pressures on their limited water resources, driven by both natural factors and human activities. The balance between supply and demand is often precarious, with little room for error or mismanagement.

One of the primary pressures is the inherently limited availability of freshwater. Small land area means there are fewer rivers, lakes, and aquifers compared to continental regions. Many islands rely almost exclusively on rainfall, which can be highly variable from year to year and increasingly unpredictable due to climate change. When rainfall is insufficient, stored water in reservoirs or tanks can quickly be depleted, leading to shortages. Groundwater resources, while vital, are often shallow and easily contaminated by saltwater intrusion, particularly as sea levels rise and as a result of over-extraction for domestic, agricultural, or tourism purposes.

Population growth and economic development add further strain to already scarce water supplies. Expanding populations increase demand for drinking water, sanitation, food production, and industry. On many islands, the tourism sector is a significant driver of economic activity, but it can place disproportionate pressure on local water systems, especially during peak seasons when the influx of visitors may double or even triple the resident population. Agriculture, another vital sector, often requires substantial amounts of water for irrigation, further competing with other needs.

Pollution is an additional challenge affecting both water quality and quantity. Inadequate wastewater treatment and poorly managed solid waste disposal can lead to contamination of both surface and groundwater resources. Agricultural runoff containing fertilizers and pesticides poses a threat to water supplies, as do oil spills, leaks from fuel storage, and other sources of industrial pollution. In densely settled or low-lying areas, septic systems and latrines can also contribute to microbial contamination, posing health risks to communities that rely on local water sources.

The physical landscape of small islands, often characterized by steep terrain and limited soil depth, exacerbates the difficulty of storing water and capturing runoff for later use. During heavy rains, water can quickly run off to the sea, reducing the opportunity for replenishing groundwater or filling reservoirs. Conversely, during dry periods, the lack of storage capacity becomes a major constraint, heightening the risk of water scarcity.

Lastly, institutional and technical challenges play a significant role in shaping water resource pressures. Limited budgets, gaps in technical expertise, and fragmented governance can hinder the effective management, monitoring, and maintenance of water infrastructure. In many cases, traditional knowledge and informal management practices remain important but may not be sufficient to address contemporary challenges.

Together, these pressures create a situation where water security is a daily concern for small island communities. Ensuring reliable and safe access to water requires a coordinated approach that addresses both natural limitations and the increasing demands of modern life, while also protecting resources from pollution and overuse.

1.4 Key Barriers to Adaptation

Adapting to climate change and securing water resources on small islands is a formidable task, complicated by a range of barriers that limit the effectiveness and sustainability of adaptation efforts. These barriers are both structural and systemic, influencing every stage from planning to implementation.

One major barrier is limited financial capacity. Small islands often have constrained national budgets, with competing priorities across sectors such as health, education, and infrastructure. The high costs of developing, upgrading, and maintaining water systems are often beyond the means of local governments, making them reliant on external funding from donors, development banks, or international organizations. This dependence can delay urgent projects and introduce uncertainty into long-term adaptation planning.

Technical and infrastructural limitations present another significant challenge. Many small islands lack advanced water infrastructure, such as centralized water treatment plants, large-scale storage facilities, and robust distribution networks. Existing systems may be outdated, undersized, or poorly maintained, resulting in high levels of water loss, inefficiency, and vulnerability to extreme weather events. Furthermore, the technical expertise required to design, operate, and maintain modern water systems is often in short supply, limiting the ability of local authorities to adopt innovative solutions or respond quickly to emergencies.

Institutional and governance challenges also play a central role. Fragmented responsibilities among government agencies, unclear mandates, and weak coordination can hinder the development of integrated water management strategies. Policies may be outdated or insufficiently enforced, while bureaucratic procedures can slow down the approval and execution of adaptation initiatives. Additionally, in some cases, there is a lack of engagement with communities and key stakeholders, resulting in solutions that are not fully supported or adopted by those most affected.

Social and cultural factors can further impede adaptation. Traditional knowledge and community-based practices are valuable assets but may not always align with new technologies or approaches promoted by external actors. Resistance to change, skepticism towards outside interventions, or unequal participation of marginalized groups—such as women, youth, or indigenous peoples—can reduce the effectiveness of adaptation efforts and prevent the benefits from reaching all members of society.

Environmental and geographic constraints also shape the adaptation landscape. The small size and isolation of islands limit the scope for developing new water sources, relocating infrastructure, or diversifying supply options. Exposure to multiple and compounding hazards—such as cyclones, droughts, and sea level rise—complicates planning and stretches already limited resources. Climate change can also accelerate environmental degradation, reducing the effectiveness of existing water management practices.

Finally, data and information gaps hinder effective adaptation. Many small islands lack reliable hydrological and meteorological monitoring systems, making it difficult to assess risks, plan for future scenarios, or evaluate the success of interventions. Limited access to scientific research and technical guidance can slow the uptake of best practices and restrict innovation.

Overcoming these barriers requires coordinated action at all levels, including stronger institutional arrangements, targeted investment, capacity building, and the meaningful involvement of local communities. Only through addressing these underlying challenges can small islands make lasting progress towards climate resilience and water security.

1.5 The Urgency of Building Resilience

Building resilience in small islands is no longer a matter of long-term planning—it is an immediate necessity. The pace and scale of climate change are accelerating, and its impacts are unfolding with increasing frequency and intensity, making the need for proactive measures more urgent than ever. Small islands, with their unique vulnerabilities and constrained resources, stand at a crossroads where decisive action will determine their future sustainability and the wellbeing of their populations.

The urgency is driven first by the direct threats to water security. Every year, more islands experience periods of acute water scarcity due to prolonged droughts, reduced rainfall, or the loss of freshwater sources to saltwater intrusion. The inability to guarantee reliable access to clean water undermines public health, food security, economic stability, and social cohesion. For many communities, recurring water shortages force reliance on expensive imports, rationing, or unsafe alternatives, creating additional hardship and exacerbating inequality.

Rapid environmental changes further amplify risks. Sea level rise and coastal erosion are advancing at rates that outpace the capacity of many islands to respond with engineered or nature-based solutions. Storms and extreme weather events have become more frequent and intense, overwhelming existing infrastructure and causing long-term damage that is difficult and costly to repair. These events can set back years of development progress in a single day, reinforcing the critical need for systems that can withstand shocks and recover quickly.

The social and economic implications are profound. Water insecurity disrupts education as schools struggle to remain open during shortages, impacts health through the spread of waterborne diseases, and limits livelihoods in agriculture, fisheries, and tourism. The cumulative stress can also drive out-migration, leading to the loss of traditional knowledge, social capital, and labor that are essential for community resilience. The loss of cultural and ecological assets threatens not only individual islands but also the shared heritage and biodiversity of entire regions.

At the international level, there is growing recognition that the experiences of small islands offer early warning signals for global climate risks. The solutions developed and lessons learned in these contexts can inform adaptation efforts elsewhere, providing models for resilience in other vulnerable regions. However, time is short, and the window for effective intervention is rapidly closing as the costs of inaction rise.

Resilience building is not simply about resisting change; it is about creating adaptive systems that can anticipate, absorb, and recover from disruptions while maintaining essential functions. This requires integrating traditional knowledge with new technologies, strengthening governance, improving data and monitoring, and mobilizing investment for innovative solutions. It also demands the active involvement of communities in shaping their own futures, ensuring that adaptation strategies are grounded in local realities and aspirations.

The challenge is great, but so too is the opportunity. By prioritizing resilience now, small islands can protect their people, economies, and environments, positioning themselves as leaders in climate adaptation and sustainable development. The urgency of building resilience is clear—failure to act risks irreversible loss, while decisive action offers a pathway to a more secure and thriving future.

Chapter 2: Water Sources and Water Security in Small Islands

Water security is a persistent and pressing concern for small islands, where freshwater resources are scarce, fragile, and highly vulnerable to environmental and human pressures. The range and reliability of available water sources—rainwater, groundwater, surface water, and increasingly, desalination—are shaped by unique island geographies, climates, and social dynamics. Securing adequate, safe, and sustainable supplies requires an understanding of how these sources interact, the factors that influence their availability and quality, and the challenges posed by climate change, population growth, and development. This chapter provides a comprehensive overview of the main water sources found on small islands, explores the complex pressures that threaten their sustainability, and discusses the integrated approaches needed to build lasting water security. By examining both the opportunities and constraints, we can better identify practical solutions to support resilient island communities.

2.1 Overview of Island Water Sources

Small islands rely on a limited and often fragile mix of water sources to meet the needs of their populations, economies, and ecosystems. The availability, reliability, and quality of these sources are shaped by the unique geographic, climatic, and geologic conditions of each island, as well as by human use and management. Understanding the main sources of freshwater is essential for designing effective strategies to ensure water security and build resilience against climate change.

The most common and traditional source of freshwater on small islands is rainwater harvesting. Given the absence of large rivers and lakes, many islands depend on direct collection and storage of rainwater from rooftops, paved surfaces, or purpose-built catchments. Rainwater is typically captured during the wet season and stored in tanks or cisterns for use during dry periods. This method is cost-effective and sustainable, but it is vulnerable to prolonged droughts or changes in precipitation patterns, which can reduce the amount of water available.

Groundwater is another critical source, usually found in the form of shallow freshwater lenses that float atop denser saltwater in the porous rock or sand of island aquifers. Access to groundwater allows for year-round supply, but the volume of these lenses is often limited and highly sensitive to over-extraction and contamination. Excessive pumping can lead to saltwater intrusion, rendering the water unfit for human consumption and agriculture. Groundwater is also threatened by pollution from domestic wastewater, agricultural runoff, and stormwater infiltration.

In some islands, surface water—such as small streams, springs, or ponds—provides a portion of the supply, especially in areas with higher elevations or volcanic origins. However, the capacity of these sources is generally limited and often seasonal. Surface water systems may be susceptible to pollution, sedimentation, and evaporation losses, making them less reliable during periods of drought or extreme heat.

For islands facing severe shortages or quality issues, desalination has emerged as an increasingly important, albeit resource-intensive, option. Desalination plants use energy-intensive processes to convert seawater into potable water. While this technology offers a potentially unlimited supply and is resilient to climate-driven changes in rainfall, it is expensive to install and operate, requires significant energy inputs, and produces brine waste that must be carefully managed to avoid environmental harm.

A small number of islands, particularly those with limited freshwater resources or facing acute crises, have resorted to importing water by ship or barge from the mainland or neighboring islands. While this provides short-term relief, it is logistically challenging, costly, and unsustainable as a long-term solution.

The mix and viability of these sources depend on local conditions, such as rainfall patterns, geology, population density, and infrastructure. Many islands use a combination of these methods to meet varying needs across communities, sectors, and seasons. Effective water security planning requires a clear understanding of the strengths and limitations of each source, as well as integrated management to ensure sustainability, reliability, and resilience in the face of changing environmental and socioeconomic pressures.

2.2 Factors Influencing Water Availability and Quality

The availability and quality of water on small islands are shaped by a complex interplay of natural processes and human activities. These factors can vary significantly from one island to another, yet several common elements influence how much water is accessible, when it is available, and whether it is safe to use.

A primary factor affecting water availability is climate variability, particularly the distribution and intensity of rainfall. Most small islands are highly dependent on seasonal rains to replenish their water sources. Variations in the timing and amount of precipitation—due to phenomena such as El Niño or climate change—can lead to periods of both drought and flooding, making water supply unpredictable. Prolonged dry spells can deplete rainwater tanks and lower groundwater levels, while intense storms may cause runoff that cannot be captured or stored effectively.

Geological characteristics also play a significant role. Many islands are composed of porous limestone, volcanic rock, or coral sand, which can influence the formation and capacity of groundwater lenses and aquifers. The permeability of the ground affects how quickly water can infiltrate and be stored, as well as the risk of contamination from surface pollutants. Low-lying islands with thin soil layers are particularly vulnerable to saltwater intrusion, especially as sea levels rise and as freshwater is extracted faster than it can be naturally recharged.

Population density and patterns of land use have a direct impact on both the quantity and quality of available water. Densely populated areas place greater demand on local water sources, often leading to over-extraction of groundwater or depletion of stored rainwater. Expanding urbanization and tourism developments can increase impervious surfaces, reducing natural recharge and increasing the risk of pollution from stormwater runoff. Agricultural activities may also require significant water inputs, especially where irrigation is practiced, and can introduce fertilizers, pesticides, and other contaminants into water supplies.

Water quality is further influenced by the adequacy of wastewater management and solid waste disposal. On many islands, limited infrastructure for sewage treatment means that untreated or poorly treated effluent can enter groundwater or coastal waters, raising health risks and reducing the usability of local supplies. Inadequate solid waste management can result in leachate from landfills or dumping sites contaminating both surface and groundwater resources.

The availability of technology and infrastructure determines the ability to collect, treat, and distribute water effectively. Islands with well-developed rainwater harvesting systems, storage facilities, and efficient distribution networks are better able to manage variable supply and protect water quality. However, aging infrastructure, limited maintenance, and financial constraints can undermine these systems, resulting in high rates of leakage, inefficient usage, and increased vulnerability to climate extremes.

Finally, governance and institutional capacity are crucial in shaping water outcomes. The presence of effective policies, regulations, and management practices determines how resources are allocated, protected, and restored. Community awareness and engagement are also key, as informed and motivated residents can play an active role in conserving water and safeguarding its quality.

Collectively, these factors underscore the need for integrated and adaptive water management approaches that address the physical, social, and institutional realities of small islands. By understanding and responding to the diverse influences on water availability and quality, island communities can strengthen their resilience to both current challenges and future uncertainties.

2.3 Challenges in Water Management

Water management on small islands is characterized by a range of persistent challenges that stem from their unique geographic, environmental, and socioeconomic circumstances. These challenges complicate efforts to ensure reliable, safe, and sustainable water supply for all users, often requiring creative and context-specific solutions.

A fundamental challenge is the inherent limitation of water resources. Most small islands have little or no access to surface water, and their groundwater reserves are typically small, fragile, and highly vulnerable to over-extraction and contamination. The absence of large rivers or lakes means there are few opportunities for large-scale storage, forcing communities to rely heavily on rainwater harvesting or shallow aquifers. This reliance increases the risk of shortages during dry periods or droughts and leaves water supplies vulnerable to climate variability and change.

Seasonal and interannual variability in rainfall further complicates management. Wet seasons may bring abundant water, while dry seasons can cause prolonged scarcity. In some years, delayed or below-average rainfall can lead to severe shortages, particularly if storage systems are inadequate or not well maintained. The unpredictability of rainfall patterns, driven in part by climate change, makes it difficult to plan for future supply and demand, requiring robust monitoring and flexible management strategies.

Infrastructure constraints are another major obstacle. Many small islands operate with aging, undersized, or poorly maintained water supply systems. Leaks, losses, and inefficiencies in collection, storage, and distribution reduce the amount of water available for use. Inadequate infrastructure can also result in the mixing of potable and non-potable water, posing health risks to the population. Limited access to spare parts, skilled technicians, and financial resources often means repairs and upgrades are delayed, leading to further system degradation.

Water quality management is an ongoing concern. Pollution from wastewater, agricultural runoff, and solid waste disposal can degrade both surface and groundwater supplies. The lack of comprehensive wastewater treatment systems means that untreated sewage may be discharged directly into the environment, contaminating water sources and coastal ecosystems. Salinization, caused by saltwater intrusion or over-extraction of groundwater, is a common and growing problem, particularly in low-lying and atoll islands.

Institutional fragmentation and weak governance hinder effective water management. Responsibilities for water resources may be divided among multiple agencies, resulting in poor coordination, overlapping mandates, and inefficient allocation of resources. Outdated policies, insufficient regulation, and limited enforcement contribute to unsustainable practices and hinder the adoption of new technologies or approaches. Moreover, a lack of reliable data on water availability, quality, and usage makes evidence-based decision-making challenging.

Social and economic factors further complicate management. Rapid population growth, urbanization, and tourism expansion increase water demand, while economic limitations restrict the ability to invest in modern infrastructure and management systems. In many cases, communities lack awareness of the importance of water conservation and may not be fully engaged in planning and decision-making processes. Disparities in access to water between urban and rural areas, or between residents and tourists, can lead to social tensions and undermine efforts to build resilience.

Lastly, the isolated nature of many islands makes importing water, equipment, and technical expertise difficult and expensive. This isolation can delay responses to emergencies, slow the introduction of innovative solutions, and restrict opportunities for regional collaboration or support.

Addressing these challenges requires integrated, adaptive, and participatory water management that takes into account the specific realities of small island environments. Building local capacity, improving infrastructure, strengthening institutions, and promoting community involvement are all essential steps towards achieving water security and long-term sustainability.

2.4 Building Water Security

Building water security on small islands requires a holistic, adaptive approach that addresses both immediate needs and long-term resilience. Given the combination of limited freshwater resources, climatic variability, and socioeconomic constraints, strategies for water security must be locally relevant, sustainable, and capable of responding to changing conditions.

A foundational element in building water security is the diversification of water sources. Relying on a single source, such as rainwater or groundwater, increases vulnerability to supply disruptions from drought, contamination, or overuse. By developing a mix of water supply options—including rainwater harvesting, groundwater management, surface water use where available, and desalination—small islands can increase flexibility and reduce risk. Each source should be assessed for its reliability, environmental impact, and economic feasibility, with particular attention to sustainable withdrawal rates and maintenance requirements.

Storage capacity is another critical factor. Effective water security depends not only on the amount of water available but also on the ability to store surplus during wet periods for use during dry spells. Investing in household and community-scale storage solutions, such as tanks, cisterns, and reservoirs, helps to smooth out seasonal fluctuations and provide a buffer against unexpected shortages. Maintenance and regular inspection of storage infrastructure are essential to ensure quality and prevent losses from leaks or contamination.

Demand management is equally important. Promoting water efficiency and conservation through public education, incentives, and regulations can significantly reduce pressure on limited supplies. Simple measures, such as installing low-flow fixtures, repairing leaks, and encouraging mindful use, can have a substantial impact when widely adopted. In tourism and agriculture, adopting best practices for water use and recycling can further enhance overall efficiency.

Protecting water quality is fundamental to water security. Implementing safeguards to prevent pollution from wastewater, agriculture, and solid waste protects both human health and ecosystem function. This may involve upgrading or expanding wastewater treatment facilities, promoting safe disposal practices, and protecting recharge areas through land use planning and regulation. Regular water quality monitoring allows for early detection of contamination and timely responses to emerging threats.

Strengthening governance and institutional capacity is necessary for the effective management of water resources. Clear policies, regulations, and enforcement mechanisms should guide allocation, use, and protection of water sources. Building coordination among agencies and involving local communities in decision-making processes fosters ownership, transparency, and the development of context-specific solutions. Incorporating traditional knowledge and local experience alongside scientific research can help ensure that strategies are both effective and culturally appropriate.

Financial sustainability must also be addressed. Establishing fair and transparent pricing, exploring options for cross-subsidization, and leveraging external funding can support both the operation and long-term maintenance of water systems. Building the capacity of local authorities and communities to manage funds, plan investments, and access new sources of finance strengthens the overall resilience of the sector.

Finally, building water security requires ongoing adaptation and learning. Climate change, population shifts, and economic development all introduce new pressures and uncertainties. Regular assessment, monitoring, and adjustment of strategies allow for flexible responses and continuous improvement. By fostering a culture of innovation and preparedness, small islands can better navigate emerging challenges and protect their water resources for future generations.

Chapter 3: Integrated Water Resources Management for Small Islands

Managing water resources on small islands requires a comprehensive and coordinated approach that addresses the complexity and interconnectedness of local systems. Integrated Water Resources Management (IWRM) offers a framework to bring together all water sources, users, and stakeholders in pursuit of sustainable and equitable outcomes. For small islands, where natural and human factors interact intensely and vulnerabilities are acute, IWRM helps to overcome fragmented management and enables adaptive, participatory, and evidence-based decision-making. This chapter introduces the core principles and practical tools of IWRM, examines their relevance in the island context, and discusses the challenges and opportunities for implementation. By exploring pathways to integrate policy, planning, and community engagement, we set the stage for more resilient and efficient management of scarce water resources under conditions of growing uncertainty.

3.1 Principles of IWRM in Island Contexts

IWRM provides a framework for addressing the complexity and interconnectedness of water challenges, and its principles are particularly relevant for small island contexts. The goal of IWRM is to coordinate the development and management of water, land, and related resources to maximize social and economic welfare without compromising the sustainability of vital ecosystems. On small islands, where water resources are scarce, fragile, and closely linked with other environmental and societal systems, the adoption of IWRM principles is essential for effective and resilient water management.

A core principle of IWRM is the integration of all water sources, uses, and users within a single management framework. For small islands, this means considering rainwater, groundwater, surface water, desalinated water, and even imported supplies together, rather than in isolation. Management should account for domestic, agricultural, industrial, and tourism needs, as well as environmental requirements. Recognizing the competing and complementary demands across sectors enables more balanced and equitable allocation, helping to avoid over-extraction, pollution, and conflict.

Participation and stakeholder engagement are also fundamental to IWRM. Small island communities are often closely knit, and involving local residents, businesses, traditional leaders, and civil society organizations in decision-making ensures that management approaches reflect local knowledge, needs, and priorities. Genuine participation fosters transparency, trust, and a sense of ownership, which are critical for the success and sustainability of water management interventions. Mechanisms for community consultation, education, and feedback should be built into all stages of planning and implementation.

Another important principle is the integration of land and water management. On small islands, land use decisions—such as zoning, urban development, agriculture, and conservation—directly affect water availability, quality, and recharge. Coordinating land and water planning helps protect key resources like watersheds, recharge zones, and coastal areas from degradation and pollution. Strategies should promote sustainable land management practices that support water conservation, prevent erosion, and maintain the health of ecosystems that underpin water supplies.

Adaptiveness and flexibility are essential in the face of uncertainty and change. The dynamic nature of climate, population, and economic activities on small islands requires management systems that can learn from experience, adjust to new information, and respond to emerging challenges. Building in regular monitoring, evaluation, and opportunities for revision ensures that management strategies remain relevant and effective over time.

Sustainability underpins all IWRM principles. The needs of current generations must be met without jeopardizing the ability of future generations to access and benefit from water resources. On small islands, this calls for careful consideration of extraction rates, investment in infrastructure maintenance, protection of water quality, and the restoration of degraded ecosystems.

Finally, IWRM in island contexts emphasizes the importance of supportive policy and institutional frameworks. This includes clear legal mandates, coordination among agencies, and the development of technical and financial capacity at both local and national levels. Partnerships with regional and international organizations can also provide access to expertise, funding, and best practices.

Applying the principles of IWRM on small islands enables a more coherent, participatory, and sustainable approach to water management—one that addresses immediate needs while building resilience for the future.

3.2 Assessing Water Resources and Risks

Effective management of water resources on small islands begins with a comprehensive assessment of both available water supplies and the risks that threaten their sustainability. Given the limited scale and high vulnerability of island environments, such assessments are vital for informed decision-making and the development of adaptive strategies.

The first step in assessing water resources is to inventory all potential sources. This includes quantifying the amount of water that can be captured from rainfall, the storage capacity of tanks and reservoirs, the volume and recharge rates of groundwater lenses, and the output of any surface water bodies or desalination plants. Accurate measurement of these sources often requires a combination of field surveys, monitoring equipment, and historical records. In many cases, investments in modern monitoring technologies, such as remote sensors and automated data loggers, can provide real-time information to support management decisions.

Assessing water quality is equally important. Regular sampling and analysis of key parameters—such as salinity, microbiological contaminants, nutrients, and pollutants—allow managers to track changes over time and detect emerging threats. Understanding the baseline quality of water sources is essential for identifying trends, evaluating the impacts of land use and human activities, and prioritizing actions to protect public health and the environment.

A key component of risk assessment is the identification of hazards that can affect both water availability and quality. On small islands, these hazards may include drought, intense rainfall events, saltwater intrusion, contamination from wastewater or agricultural runoff, and infrastructure failures. Climate change is expected to amplify many of these risks, introducing greater variability and uncertainty into water systems. Mapping the geographic extent and severity of potential hazards—using tools such as Geographic Information Systems (GIS) and risk modeling—enables managers to target interventions more effectively.

Vulnerability assessment goes beyond the identification of hazards to consider the sensitivity and adaptive capacity of island communities and water systems. Factors such as population density, economic activity, existing infrastructure, institutional capacity, and community awareness all influence how water resources are affected by and respond to stressors. Engaging stakeholders in vulnerability assessment helps to capture local knowledge, social dynamics, and priorities that may not be evident through technical analysis alone.

Demand assessment is another important element. Understanding current and projected water use across different sectors—domestic, agricultural, industrial, and tourism—enables planners to anticipate pressures on supply and identify opportunities for conservation or demand management. Seasonal variations, peak demand periods, and the impact of special events or population shifts should all be taken into account.

Finally, integrating the findings from resource and risk assessments into planning processes ensures that management strategies are grounded in reality and responsive to actual needs and challenges. This integration can take the form of water budgets, drought contingency plans, early warning systems, and the establishment of monitoring and evaluation frameworks. Periodic reassessment is necessary to accommodate changes in climate, population, technology, and socioeconomic conditions.

By systematically assessing water resources and risks, small islands can build a solid foundation for sustainable management, improve resilience to shocks and stresses, and support the long-term security and wellbeing of their communities.

3.3 Planning and Governance

Effective planning and governance are crucial for achieving sustainable water management on small islands, where limited resources and heightened vulnerability demand strategic, coordinated, and participatory approaches. The unique context of small islands requires governance structures and planning processes that are flexible, transparent, and responsive to both local needs and external pressures.

Planning begins with the development of a clear vision and strategic objectives for water management. This involves setting priorities that reflect the realities of the island's physical environment, economic activities, and social dynamics. Comprehensive water management plans should be informed by robust data on water availability, quality, and demand, and should integrate climate risk assessments and future projections. Scenario planning and adaptive management approaches are particularly valuable, as they enable planners to respond to uncertainties and adjust strategies as conditions change.

Governance structures on small islands are often characterized by limited capacity, overlapping mandates, and resource constraints.

Strengthening these structures requires clarifying the roles and responsibilities of different institutions and agencies involved in water management, from national ministries and local governments to utilities and community organizations. Establishing clear lines of authority and effective coordination mechanisms helps to avoid duplication of effort, resolve conflicts, and promote integrated decision-making.

Transparency and accountability are essential for building public trust and ensuring the fair allocation and use of water resources. This includes developing policies and regulations that are accessible, enforceable, and regularly reviewed, as well as fostering open communication between authorities and stakeholders. Mechanisms for monitoring compliance, addressing grievances, and incorporating feedback from users are important for improving performance and adapting to evolving needs.

Participation of local communities, civil society organizations, and the private sector enhances the legitimacy and effectiveness of planning and governance. Engaging stakeholders throughout the planning process ensures that diverse perspectives and knowledge are considered, strengthens ownership of decisions, and increases the likelihood of successful implementation. Participatory approaches may include public consultations, advisory committees, and collaborative management agreements.

Regional cooperation can also play a significant role in strengthening planning and governance on small islands. Partnerships with neighboring islands, regional organizations, and international agencies can facilitate the sharing of best practices, access to technical expertise, and the mobilization of financial resources. Such cooperation is particularly valuable for addressing transboundary water issues, accessing external funding, and enhancing collective resilience to shared risks.

The success of planning and governance in small island water management depends on a commitment to long-term sustainability, equity, and adaptability. By fostering strong institutions, inclusive participation, and a culture of learning, small islands can develop water management systems that are resilient to current and future challenges.

3.4 Tools and Instruments for IWRM

The implementation of IWRM on small islands relies on a range of tools and instruments designed to support coordination, efficiency, and sustainability in water management. These tools help translate IWRM principles into practical actions and facilitate the integration of diverse water sources, uses, and stakeholders.

Water allocation frameworks are fundamental instruments for balancing competing demands across sectors such as domestic supply, agriculture, industry, and tourism. Establishing clear guidelines for water rights, priorities during scarcity, and rules for equitable distribution helps to reduce conflict and ensure that critical needs are met, even in times of stress.

Regulatory and policy tools provide the legal foundation for sustainable water use. This includes setting standards for water quality, regulating groundwater extraction, and enforcing pollution controls. Effective policies also establish requirements for infrastructure maintenance, monitoring, and reporting, supporting accountability and long-term system reliability.

Economic instruments such as tariffs, subsidies, and incentives can be used to influence water use behavior and promote conservation. Pricing structures that reflect the true cost of supply and encourage efficient use help to manage demand and generate revenue for reinvestment in water infrastructure. Subsidies or financial support may be provided for low-income households or for the adoption of water-saving technologies.

Technical tools play a crucial role in monitoring and management. These include metering and data logging systems for tracking water use, leak detection technologies to reduce losses, and GIS for mapping water resources, infrastructure, and risks. Early warning systems and real-time monitoring support rapid response to emerging challenges such as drought, contamination, or infrastructure failure.

Decision support systems integrate data from various sources to inform planning, scenario analysis, and adaptive management. By modeling different water supply and demand scenarios, these systems help managers understand trade-offs and make informed choices under uncertainty. Participatory mapping and planning tools also facilitate stakeholder engagement and ensure that local knowledge and priorities are reflected in management decisions.

Finally, capacity building instruments such as training programs, educational materials, and community workshops help to strengthen the skills and knowledge of both water professionals and users. Ongoing capacity building is vital for sustaining effective IWRM implementation and supporting the adoption of new technologies and practices.

By leveraging these tools and instruments, small islands can operationalize IWRM principles, enhance water security, and build resilience to current and future challenges.

3.5 Limitations and Pathways Forward

While IWRM offers significant benefits for small islands, there are notable limitations that can hinder its full implementation. Recognizing these challenges is essential for identifying practical pathways forward and ensuring that water management approaches remain effective and relevant.

One limitation is the constrained institutional and technical capacity on many small islands. Limited staff, expertise, and financial resources can slow progress in developing and maintaining comprehensive IWRM systems. The absence of dedicated personnel for water resource assessment, planning, and enforcement can lead to gaps in management and reduce the effectiveness of policy frameworks and regulatory tools.

Data scarcity is another persistent challenge. Reliable information on water availability, usage, and quality is often limited or unavailable, making it difficult to make evidence-based decisions or monitor the impacts of management actions. Gaps in long-term data also hinder the ability to anticipate and respond to emerging risks, especially as climate variability increases.

Social and political factors may also pose barriers. Stakeholder engagement can be limited by cultural norms, lack of awareness, or competing community priorities. Governance structures may be fragmented, with overlapping responsibilities and insufficient coordination among agencies, reducing the efficiency of integrated approaches. In addition, changing political leadership or shifting development priorities can interrupt continuity in water management efforts.

Despite these limitations, there are clear pathways forward. Investing in capacity building—through training, technical assistance, and regional collaboration—can strengthen local expertise and management capabilities. Improving data collection and sharing, including the use of new technologies and community-based monitoring, enhances the information base needed for adaptive management.

Promoting stronger stakeholder engagement and participatory processes can help ensure that diverse voices are included and that management strategies are grounded in local realities. Regional cooperation among islands can facilitate the exchange of best practices, access to funding, and joint responses to shared challenges.

By acknowledging the limitations and building on existing strengths, small islands can continue to advance IWRM, creating more resilient and sustainable water systems for the future.

Chapter 4: Building Climate-Resilient Water Infrastructure

Climate-resilient water infrastructure is essential for the survival and prosperity of small islands facing increasing environmental pressures. The ability to deliver safe, reliable water supplies depends on systems that can withstand climate extremes, adapt to changing conditions, and protect scarce freshwater resources from contamination and loss. This chapter explores the design, implementation, and maintenance of water infrastructure suited to the unique needs of small islands, including rainwater harvesting, desalination, groundwater management, and the integration of nature-based solutions. Attention is given to both technological innovation and the importance of involving local communities in planning and operation. By strengthening the physical backbone of water supply and management, small islands can reduce vulnerability, support economic development, and lay the foundation for long-term resilience in an uncertain climate future.

4.1 Design Criteria for Island Water Systems

Designing effective water systems for small islands requires careful consideration of local environmental, social, and economic conditions. Given the limited resources and unique vulnerabilities faced by island communities, water systems must be tailored to ensure reliability, resilience, and sustainability. The following criteria are essential for guiding the design and implementation of water infrastructure on small islands.

The first criterion is climate and hazard resilience. Water systems must be able to withstand and function during extreme weather events such as tropical storms, cyclones, and prolonged droughts. This includes ensuring that storage tanks, pipelines, and treatment facilities are robust enough to resist wind, flooding, and saltwater intrusion. Elevating and protecting key infrastructure, designing systems with backup capacity, and incorporating redundancy help reduce the risk of service interruptions during emergencies.

Adaptability to variable water supply is another important criterion. Given the seasonality and unpredictability of rainfall on many islands, water systems should be designed with flexible intake and storage options. This might involve modular storage tanks that can be expanded, multiple water source connections, or the ability to switch between rainwater, groundwater, and desalinated supply as conditions demand. Systems should also allow for gradual upgrades as population and demand change over time.

Water quality protection must be a core design principle. Infrastructure should minimize the risk of contamination at every stage—from collection and storage to treatment and distribution. This includes using non-corrosive and food-grade materials, designing tanks and reservoirs to prevent algae growth and mosquito breeding, and ensuring effective barriers against intrusion by saltwater or pollutants. Integration of filtration and disinfection systems supports the delivery of safe drinking water even during challenging conditions.

Efficiency and minimizing water loss are critical for making the most of scarce resources. Systems should be designed to reduce leakage, evaporation, and other forms of loss. This may involve using high-quality pipes and fittings, incorporating leak detection and repair protocols, and placing storage as close as possible to points of use. Demand management features, such as pressure regulators and flow restrictors, can help conserve water and prevent waste.

Social acceptability and community involvement are vital for long-term success. Water system designs should reflect local preferences, customs, and knowledge, ensuring that technology choices are user-friendly and maintainable with available skills and resources. Involving communities in planning, construction, and maintenance builds ownership, encourages care for infrastructure, and enhances sustainability.

Lastly, financial and operational sustainability must be considered from the outset. Systems should be affordable to construct, operate, and maintain, with clear arrangements for cost recovery, budgeting, and technical support. Simple, robust designs that require minimal specialized parts or expertise are often best suited to small island contexts.

By adhering to these design criteria, small islands can develop water systems that are robust, adaptable, and capable of supporting their communities now and into the future.

4.2 Rainwater Harvesting Systems

Rainwater harvesting systems are a vital component of water supply strategies on small islands, offering a decentralized and sustainable way to capture and store freshwater. Due to the limited availability of surface water and the vulnerability of groundwater sources, rainwater collection is often the most accessible and reliable method for meeting household, community, and even institutional water needs. Designing and maintaining effective rainwater harvesting systems requires attention to both technical specifications and the broader context of island environments.

The basic components of a rainwater harvesting system include a catchment surface, conveyance infrastructure, storage tanks, and treatment measures. The catchment is typically the roof of a building, constructed from materials such as metal or tile that are smooth and non-toxic, allowing rain to flow freely and minimizing contamination. Gutters and downspouts channel rainwater from the catchment to storage tanks, which can vary in size and material depending on available space, rainfall patterns, and budget. Polyethylene, concrete, and fiberglass are common tank materials, selected for durability and suitability to the local climate.

Sizing of storage tanks is a critical design consideration. Tanks should be large enough to store sufficient water to bridge dry spells or periods of high demand, taking into account local rainfall variability, roof area, and intended water uses. In some cases, modular or interconnected tanks can offer flexibility, allowing for phased expansion as needs change or as funds become available. Proper tank placement and secure foundations reduce the risk of contamination or damage from storms and flooding.

Ensuring water quality is a key aspect of system design. First-flush diverters are used to discard the initial runoff from a rain event, which may contain dust, leaves, or other debris from the roof. Simple screens and filters in gutters and at the tank inlet help keep out insects, rodents, and larger particles. Regular cleaning and maintenance of catchments, gutters, and tanks are essential to prevent the buildup of contaminants and algae. Where rainwater is used for drinking, additional treatment such as filtration, disinfection, or boiling may be necessary to meet health standards.

Community-scale rainwater harvesting systems can be implemented in schools, health centers, and other public buildings, providing a valuable resource during droughts or supply interruptions. These systems can also play a critical role in disaster preparedness, offering backup water supplies when centralized infrastructure is disrupted.

Economic and social factors should guide system design and management. Affordability is key, so simple, low-cost technologies that can be maintained locally are preferred. Community involvement in planning, installation, and upkeep fosters a sense of ownership and ensures that systems are tailored to local needs and practices. Public education on the benefits and proper use of rainwater harvesting enhances system acceptance and sustainability.

Overall, rainwater harvesting systems, when well designed and maintained, provide a reliable, cost-effective, and climate-resilient water supply solution for small islands. They offer a practical means of bridging supply gaps, supporting adaptation to changing rainfall patterns, and building long-term water security.

4.3 Desalination Technologies

Desalination technologies have become an increasingly important option for securing water supply on small islands, especially those facing chronic shortages or limited freshwater resources. The ability to convert abundant seawater into potable water offers a potential solution to the constraints of rainfall variability, over-exploited aquifers, and population growth. However, the adoption of desalination requires careful consideration of technical, economic, and environmental factors to ensure its viability and sustainability in island contexts.

The most widely used desalination technology on small islands is reverse osmosis. This process uses high-pressure pumps to force seawater through semi-permeable membranes that separate salts and impurities from water molecules, producing fresh water on one side and a concentrated brine on the other. Reverse osmosis systems are favored for their relatively compact footprint, modular design, and ability to produce high-quality water suitable for drinking and other uses. Advances in membrane materials and energy recovery technologies have made these systems more efficient and cost-effective in recent years.

Other desalination methods, such as multi-stage flash distillation or electrodialysis, are less common on small islands due to higher capital costs, greater energy requirements, or greater operational complexity. Solar-powered or hybrid desalination systems are being explored in some locations as a means of reducing reliance on imported fuels and minimizing environmental impacts, but these approaches are typically limited to small-scale or pilot applications.

Energy use is a central consideration for all desalination technologies. Producing fresh water from seawater is energy-intensive, and on many small islands, electricity is generated from imported fossil fuels. This can make desalinated water expensive and increase greenhouse gas emissions, potentially conflicting with broader sustainability goals. Integrating renewable energy sources, such as solar or wind, can help lower operational costs and environmental impacts, though initial investments may be high.

Managing the environmental impacts of desalination is also critical. The disposal of concentrated brine, a byproduct of the desalination process, can harm marine ecosystems if not properly managed. Best practices include diluting brine with other waste streams, dispersing it over a wide area, or using it for secondary applications where feasible. Careful site selection, design of outfall structures, and ongoing monitoring help mitigate risks to coral reefs, fisheries, and coastal habitats.

Operational reliability and maintenance present additional challenges. Desalination plants require skilled personnel for routine operation, monitoring, and maintenance, including regular cleaning or replacement of membranes and pumps. Access to spare parts and technical support can be limited on remote islands, making capacity building and supplier relationships essential.

Finally, the financial sustainability of desalination projects must be carefully evaluated. High upfront costs, ongoing energy expenses, and the need for skilled operators can strain local budgets. Cost recovery mechanisms, such as water tariffs or subsidies, should be designed to balance affordability with the need for long-term maintenance and system upgrades.

Despite these challenges, desalination offers a lifeline for small islands struggling to meet growing water needs. When integrated thoughtfully into a broader water management strategy, it can enhance resilience, diversify supply, and provide a dependable source of clean water, especially in times of drought or emergency.

4.4 Groundwater Management

Groundwater plays a critical role in supporting water security on many small islands, often serving as the main or only source of fresh water for domestic, agricultural, and industrial needs. However, the management of groundwater resources on islands presents unique challenges due to limited aquifer capacity, susceptibility to contamination, and increasing pressures from population growth and climate change. Effective groundwater management is essential for ensuring long-term sustainability and resilience.

A defining feature of groundwater on small islands is the presence of freshwater lenses—shallow bodies of fresh water that float above denser saltwater within porous rocks or coral sand. These lenses are particularly fragile and can be easily disrupted by over-extraction or sea level rise. Excessive pumping reduces the thickness of the lens, drawing in saltwater and leading to salinization that can render the water unfit for consumption or irrigation. Careful monitoring of extraction rates and well locations is required to prevent overuse and maintain the delicate balance between recharge and withdrawal.

Protecting groundwater quality is equally important. Pollution from untreated wastewater, agricultural chemicals, fuel spills, and stormwater runoff can rapidly degrade groundwater supplies, particularly in areas with thin soils or high permeability. Preventive measures include zoning regulations that restrict high-risk activities near recharge areas, the development and enforcement of standards for wastewater treatment and disposal, and the use of buffer zones around wells and aquifers. Regular water quality testing enables early detection of contamination and timely intervention.

Groundwater recharge is a crucial component of management strategies. Preserving natural recharge zones, such as forests, wetlands, and permeable open spaces, allows rainwater to infiltrate and replenish aquifers. In some cases, artificial recharge techniques—such as constructing infiltration basins or directing stormwater runoff into recharge wells—can enhance natural processes and help offset declines in groundwater levels during periods of drought or increased demand.

Data collection and monitoring underpin all aspects of groundwater management. Installing observation wells, automated sensors, and conducting regular surveys provide valuable information on water levels, quality, and usage trends. This data supports adaptive management and enables authorities to respond quickly to emerging threats, such as saltwater intrusion during storms or contamination following infrastructure failures.

Community engagement and education are essential for successful groundwater management. Island residents, farmers, and businesses need to understand the importance of protecting groundwater and the consequences of overuse or pollution. Awareness campaigns, participatory monitoring programs, and the inclusion of local stakeholders in planning processes foster collective responsibility and help ensure that management measures are respected and maintained.

Finally, groundwater management should be integrated with broader water resource planning, including the diversification of water supply sources and investment in infrastructure for rainwater harvesting, desalination, or water reuse. Reducing reliance on groundwater alone enhances resilience and helps safeguard this critical resource for future generations.

Through careful monitoring, pollution prevention, and community involvement, small islands can preserve the quality and availability of groundwater, providing a secure and reliable foundation for their water needs in an uncertain and changing climate.

4.5 Infrastructure Upgrades and Nature-Based Solutions

Upgrading water infrastructure and integrating nature-based solutions are essential strategies for strengthening water security and climate resilience on small islands. Many islands operate with aging or inadequate infrastructure, leaving them vulnerable to supply disruptions, water losses, and contamination. At the same time, working with natural systems offers opportunities to enhance water availability, improve quality, and reduce disaster risks in ways that are sustainable and cost-effective.

Infrastructure upgrades begin with modernizing existing water supply, storage, and distribution systems. Replacing old pipes, fittings, and pumps helps reduce leaks and non-revenue water, ensuring that more of the collected or treated water reaches end users. Upgrading treatment facilities allows for better removal of contaminants, providing safer water and reducing health risks. Improving storage capacity—by expanding tanks, reservoirs, or cisterns—enables communities to capture and retain more water during periods of abundance for use during dry spells or emergencies.

Smart technology and remote monitoring tools can further increase system efficiency and reliability. Installing automated sensors, leak detection systems, and data loggers helps utilities track usage, identify problems quickly, and optimize maintenance schedules. In areas where access to technical expertise is limited, investing in simple, robust designs that are easy to maintain and repair is especially important.

Nature-based solutions complement traditional infrastructure by harnessing the power of natural processes to manage water and build resilience. Restoring or protecting forests, wetlands, and mangroves supports natural water filtration, enhances groundwater recharge, and buffers against flooding and coastal erosion. Green infrastructure—such as permeable pavements, rain gardens, and vegetated swales—captures and filters stormwater, reduces runoff, and replenishes aquifers.

Rainwater infiltration systems, including soak pits and infiltration trenches, direct excess rainwater back into the ground, reducing surface runoff and helping maintain groundwater supplies. Buffer zones of native vegetation around water bodies and recharge areas filter pollutants, stabilize soil, and provide habitat for local biodiversity.

Combining infrastructure upgrades with nature-based approaches can offer multiple co-benefits. For example, integrating green roofs or urban gardens into public buildings enhances rainwater capture, improves insulation, and provides recreational or educational spaces. In coastal zones, the restoration of mangroves or coral reefs not only helps protect freshwater resources from saltwater intrusion but also supports fisheries and tourism.

Community involvement is vital in both upgrading infrastructure and implementing nature-based solutions. Engaging local residents in planning, construction, and ongoing maintenance builds local capacity, ensures the sustainability of interventions, and fosters a sense of stewardship for shared resources.

Overall, the joint pursuit of modern infrastructure and nature-based solutions provides small islands with a flexible, adaptive toolkit for addressing current challenges and preparing for future uncertainties. By investing in both engineered and natural assets, island communities can secure safer, more resilient water systems and enhance their capacity to thrive in a changing climate.

Chapter 5: Managing Water Demand and Reducing Losses

Effectively managing water demand and minimizing losses are fundamental strategies for safeguarding water security on small islands. With limited freshwater resources and increasing pressures from population growth, tourism, and climate change, it is essential to use available water as efficiently as possible. This chapter examines the patterns of water use across different sectors, identifies key drivers of demand, and explores a range of approaches to improve efficiency and conservation. Focus is placed on practical strategies, including public education, technological innovations, leak detection, and regulatory measures that help reduce waste and stretch existing supplies further. By prioritizing demand management and loss reduction, small islands can make significant strides toward resilient, sustainable water systems capable of withstanding present and future challenges.

5.1 Water Demand Patterns in Small Islands

Understanding water demand patterns is essential for effective water management on small islands, where resources are limited and supply is often vulnerable to climatic variability. Water demand on small islands is shaped by a range of factors, including population size, settlement patterns, economic activities, tourism, and seasonal fluctuations. These factors collectively influence how, when, and where water is used, often placing significant pressure on available supplies.

Domestic water use is typically the largest single component of demand on most small islands. This includes water for drinking, cooking, cleaning, bathing, laundry, and sanitation. The per capita domestic water demand can vary widely, depending on local customs, climate, levels of economic development, and the reliability of supply. In some communities, water use may be constrained by scarcity or intermittent supply, leading to lower per capita consumption and the adoption of water-saving practices as a necessity rather than a choice.

Agriculture, though often limited in scale on small islands due to land constraints, can be a significant water user where it exists. Irrigation of crops, watering of livestock, and processing of agricultural products all require substantial volumes of water. The type of crops grown, irrigation methods used, and seasonality of production influence the overall agricultural demand. In some islands, reliance on imported food has reduced agricultural water use, while others maintain intensive local production that increases competition for limited water resources.

Tourism is a major driver of water demand in many island economies. Tourist accommodations such as hotels, resorts, and guesthouses typically require large volumes of water for guest services, swimming pools, landscaping, and maintenance. During peak tourist seasons, water demand can surge dramatically, sometimes doubling or tripling the island's population equivalent. This creates significant pressure on local supply systems and can lead to shortages or competition with local residents for access to water.

Commercial and institutional water use, including businesses, schools, hospitals, and government facilities, adds to total demand. While generally smaller in scale than domestic or tourism demand, these users are essential for community function and resilience, particularly during emergencies.

Seasonal variations in demand are common. Water use tends to increase during dry seasons or droughts, as households and businesses rely more heavily on stored supplies or alternative sources. Festivals, holidays, and special events can also create temporary spikes in water consumption.

Population growth, urbanization, and changes in lifestyle or economic activity can increase long-term demand. Even modest increases in population or new development projects can strain already stretched water systems, particularly if not matched by investments in supply infrastructure and management capacity.

Understanding these demand patterns allows for better planning and management of water resources. It enables the design of targeted interventions, such as demand management programs, water conservation campaigns, and investment in supply diversification, to ensure that all sectors can access the water they need without compromising the sustainability of island water systems.

5.2 Water Efficiency and Conservation Strategies

Promoting water efficiency and conservation is crucial for small islands, where limited freshwater resources are highly sensitive to fluctuations in climate, population, and economic activity. Reducing water wastage and maximizing the productive use of each drop helps ensure that the needs of households, businesses, and the environment are met, even under conditions of scarcity or drought. Implementing a range of strategies at the household, community, and institutional levels supports both immediate and long-term water security.

One of the most effective approaches to water efficiency is public education and awareness. Informing residents, visitors, and businesses about the importance of water conservation encourages behavioral changes such as shorter showers, turning off taps while brushing teeth, and promptly repairing leaks. Outreach programs, signage, and community campaigns can be tailored to local customs and languages to ensure broad engagement and understanding.

Adopting water-saving technologies is another key strategy. Installing low-flow faucets, showerheads, and toilets reduces water use without compromising comfort or hygiene. Appliances such as washing machines and dishwashers with high-efficiency ratings further lower household consumption. In hotels and commercial buildings, retrofitting plumbing systems with water-saving devices and using automatic shut-off valves or sensor-based fixtures can make a significant difference.

Landscape and garden irrigation practices are often a major source of water use, especially in tourist areas or during dry seasons. Shifting to drought-tolerant native plants, using mulches to retain soil moisture, and watering gardens during cooler times of the day all contribute to more efficient outdoor water use. Drip irrigation and rainwater harvesting for gardens are practical options for reducing reliance on potable water for landscaping.

Leak detection and repair are essential for minimizing water losses. Utilities should regularly monitor distribution networks for leaks using acoustic sensors or pressure monitoring systems and address identified problems promptly. At the household and business level, regular checks for dripping taps, leaking toilets, or faulty pipes can prevent substantial water loss over time.

Regulatory and incentive-based measures can reinforce conservation efforts. Implementing tiered water pricing, where higher usage is charged at higher rates, encourages users to stay within reasonable limits. Offering rebates or subsidies for the purchase of water-efficient appliances, fixtures, or rainwater tanks can further motivate individuals and businesses to adopt conservation practices.

Engaging the tourism sector is particularly important for islands where visitors account for a large share of water demand. Providing information about conservation practices in hotels, encouraging towel and linen reuse, and installing water-saving devices in guest rooms are effective ways to reduce water use without compromising guest satisfaction.

A combination of public awareness, technological improvements, proactive management, and supportive policies is needed to foster a culture of water conservation. By making efficiency a shared priority, small islands can stretch limited resources further and build resilience against current and future water challenges.

5.3 Leak Detection and Non-Revenue Water

Leak detection and the reduction of non-revenue water are critical components of sustainable water management on small islands, where every drop of water counts. Non-revenue water refers to water that is produced and enters the distribution system but is lost before it reaches the customer, due to leaks, theft, metering inaccuracies, or unauthorized consumption. High levels of non-revenue water not only waste precious resources but also reduce the financial sustainability of water utilities and hinder efforts to provide reliable service.

Leaks are a primary cause of water loss in many island water supply systems, particularly where infrastructure is aging or poorly maintained. Old or corroded pipes, faulty joints, and poorly constructed connections can develop small leaks that may go undetected for long periods. Even minor leaks can result in substantial losses over time, especially in systems with high water pressure or long distribution networks. Saltwater corrosion, shifting soils, and extreme weather events can further compromise pipe integrity and increase the risk of leaks.

Detecting and repairing leaks requires a proactive and systematic approach. Utilities can implement routine monitoring programs that include acoustic sensors, pressure testing, and visual inspections to identify leaks in the distribution network. Acoustic leak detection devices are especially useful, as they can pinpoint the sound of water escaping from pipes even when the leak is not visible above ground. Pressure management systems can help identify abnormal drops in pressure that may indicate hidden leaks or bursts.

In addition to technological tools, staff training is essential for effective leak detection and repair. Field crews should be equipped with the skills and resources to promptly locate and fix leaks, as well as to document incidents and maintain accurate records. Encouraging residents and businesses to report visible leaks or unexplained wet areas in public spaces also enhances early detection and community involvement.

Non-revenue water is also caused by metering inaccuracies and unauthorized consumption. Faulty or outdated water meters can under-record usage, while connections made without proper authorization bypass billing systems. Regular meter testing, calibration, and replacement are necessary to maintain measurement accuracy. Establishing robust policies and enforcement mechanisms helps prevent illegal connections and ensures that all water users are accounted for.

Quantifying and reducing non-revenue water improves both water conservation and utility performance. Lowering losses increases the amount of water available for legitimate use, delays the need for costly supply expansions, and enhances the financial viability of water systems by improving revenue collection. Transparent reporting and regular public updates on progress can build trust and support from the community.

Addressing leaks and non-revenue water is a shared responsibility involving utilities, governments, and water users. By investing in modern technologies, capacity building, and effective policies, small islands can make substantial gains in efficiency, protect scarce resources, and ensure the long-term sustainability of their water supply systems.

5.4 Technology for Demand Management

Technology plays an increasingly important role in managing water demand on small islands, offering innovative solutions to monitor usage, detect inefficiencies, and encourage conservation. As islands face mounting pressures on limited water resources, adopting new technologies can help optimize consumption, reduce losses, and ensure that supply keeps pace with demand in a sustainable manner.

One of the most significant advancements in demand management is the use of smart water meters. Unlike traditional meters, smart meters provide real-time data on water usage at the household, commercial, or community level. These meters can transmit usage information to utilities and consumers through wireless networks, enabling users to monitor their consumption patterns, identify unusual spikes, and adjust behaviors accordingly. Utilities benefit from the ability to detect leaks, manage billing more accurately, and analyze consumption trends for better planning.

Automated meter reading (AMR) and advanced metering infrastructure (AMI) extend the benefits of smart metering by allowing remote data collection and integration with central management systems. These technologies reduce the need for manual meter reading, lower operational costs, and provide timely information for both consumers and water managers. They can also support dynamic pricing models, where water rates vary based on usage or time of day, incentivizing users to shift consumption away from peak periods.

Leak detection technologies are another valuable tool for demand management. Sensors placed along pipelines, in storage tanks, or at key points in the distribution network can provide continuous monitoring for signs of leaks or bursts. Acoustic sensors, pressure loggers, and flow meters can quickly alert operators to anomalies, allowing for rapid response and minimizing water losses. Some systems can even send automated alerts to consumers if leaks are detected within individual properties.

Water-efficient appliances and fixtures are also an important technological component. The availability of low-flow taps, toilets, showerheads, and irrigation systems enables users to reduce consumption without sacrificing performance or comfort. Smart irrigation controllers, which adjust watering schedules based on weather forecasts or soil moisture sensors, help prevent overwatering and save significant volumes of water, particularly in gardens and landscaped areas.

Mobile applications and online platforms further enhance demand management by providing consumers with access to their water usage data, conservation tips, and interactive tools. These apps can send alerts about high usage, offer comparisons with average consumption, and suggest customized actions for saving water. Educational campaigns delivered through digital channels can reach a broad audience, reinforcing the importance of efficiency and encouraging community-wide participation.

Integrating these technologies requires initial investment and ongoing support, but the benefits are substantial. Improved demand management leads to greater supply reliability, reduced strain on infrastructure, and enhanced capacity to cope with droughts or population growth. For small islands, embracing technology is a forward-looking strategy that builds resilience, empowers users, and protects vital water resources for future generations.

5.5 Achieving Sustainable Consumption

Achieving sustainable water consumption is a fundamental goal for small islands facing the twin pressures of limited resources and growing demand. Sustainable consumption means using water efficiently, minimizing waste, and ensuring that present needs are met without compromising the ability of future generations to access safe and sufficient water. This requires a combination of behavioral change, effective management, and supportive policy frameworks that together foster a culture of conservation and responsibility.

Behavioral change is at the heart of sustainable consumption. Residents, businesses, and visitors must recognize the value of water and the challenges unique to island environments. Awareness campaigns, education programs, and community engagement initiatives can inform people about the importance of conserving water and the practical steps they can take in daily life. Encouraging habits such as taking shorter showers, fixing leaks promptly, using water-efficient appliances, and reusing water where possible all contribute to a collective reduction in consumption.

Effective management by utilities and local authorities is essential for guiding and supporting sustainable use. This includes maintaining infrastructure to minimize losses, investing in leak detection, and upgrading systems to reduce inefficiencies. Regular monitoring of consumption patterns helps identify areas where interventions are needed, such as targeting high-use sectors or addressing peak demand during tourist seasons. Transparent communication about supply constraints, water quality, and the benefits of conservation builds trust and motivates compliance with conservation measures.

Policy frameworks play a critical role in enabling and enforcing sustainable consumption. Regulations that set standards for water use, mandate the installation of efficient fixtures, and require water-saving practices in new developments establish clear expectations. Pricing mechanisms, such as tiered tariffs, encourage users to stay within reasonable limits while ensuring that water remains affordable for essential needs. Incentives for adopting water-saving technologies and penalties for excessive or wasteful use provide additional motivation for change.

Community participation strengthens the effectiveness and resilience of sustainable consumption initiatives. Involving residents in planning, decision-making, and monitoring creates a sense of ownership and accountability. Local leaders, schools, and organizations can champion conservation efforts and model best practices. When the community is actively engaged, the adoption of new technologies and behaviors is faster and more enduring.

Sustainable consumption also benefits from the integration of traditional knowledge and practices. Many island communities have a long history of managing scarce water resources through collective action, seasonal rotation, or customary restrictions. Reviving and adapting these approaches to modern contexts can reinforce conservation messages and ensure that solutions are culturally appropriate.

Achieving sustainable consumption on small islands is an ongoing process that requires commitment, collaboration, and adaptability. By prioritizing efficiency, fostering community involvement, and embedding conservation in policies and daily life, small islands can secure their water future while supporting broader goals of sustainability and resilience.

Chapter 6: Protecting and Sustaining Water Quality

Protecting and sustaining water quality is a critical challenge for small islands, where limited freshwater resources are easily threatened by contamination from both natural and human sources. The health of island communities and ecosystems depends on maintaining clean, safe water supplies amidst pressures from inadequate wastewater treatment, agricultural runoff, saltwater intrusion, and extreme weather events. This chapter explores the various threats to water quality, outlines monitoring and assessment strategies, and reviews treatment options suited to island conditions. It also highlights the importance of safeguarding watersheds and recharge areas, and emphasizes the role of community engagement in maintaining high water quality standards. By addressing both prevention and remediation, small islands can secure safe water for their populations and support long-term resilience and sustainability.

6.1 Threats to Water Quality in Small Islands

Water quality is a central concern for small islands, where limited freshwater resources are easily compromised by a range of natural and human-induced threats. Ensuring safe and reliable water requires careful management to address the diverse sources of contamination that can impact both groundwater and surface water supplies.

One of the most significant threats to water quality on small islands is saltwater intrusion. Due to their proximity to the ocean and the shallow nature of freshwater lenses, small islands are especially vulnerable to the movement of saltwater into aquifers. Over-extraction of groundwater, rising sea levels, and storm surges can accelerate this process, leading to increased salinity that makes water unsuitable for drinking, agriculture, or industrial use. Once saline intrusion occurs, it can be very difficult and costly to reverse.

Pollution from inadequate wastewater treatment and sewage disposal is another major challenge. Many small islands lack comprehensive sewage infrastructure, resulting in untreated or partially treated wastewater being discharged into the environment. Leachate from septic tanks, pit latrines, and informal disposal sites can seep into groundwater or flow into surface water bodies, introducing pathogens, nutrients, and other contaminants. This can cause outbreaks of waterborne diseases and contribute to the eutrophication of lakes, lagoons, and coastal waters.

Agricultural activities also threaten water quality, particularly where fertilizers, pesticides, and herbicides are used. Runoff from agricultural fields can carry these chemicals into nearby water sources, causing nutrient enrichment, algal blooms, and toxic contamination. Livestock operations can further contribute to microbial pollution and nutrient loading, especially during heavy rains when manure is washed into streams or recharge areas.

Solid waste management poses additional risks. Inadequate collection and disposal of household and industrial waste can result in open dumping or poorly designed landfills. Rainfall can leach chemicals and pathogens from waste into the soil and groundwater, while wind-blown debris can clog drainage systems and increase flooding risks.

Stormwater runoff is a common vector for pollutants on small islands, especially in urbanized or densely populated areas. As rainwater flows over roofs, roads, and other impervious surfaces, it picks up oil, grease, heavy metals, and other contaminants, which are then transported into water bodies. The lack of green spaces and effective drainage systems exacerbates this problem, increasing the risk of flash flooding and rapid transport of pollutants.

Natural hazards such as cyclones, floods, and landslides can disrupt water quality by damaging infrastructure, mobilizing sediments, and spreading contaminants. These events can overwhelm existing water treatment and supply systems, making it difficult to maintain safe water during and after emergencies.

Lastly, emerging contaminants such as pharmaceuticals, personal care products, and microplastics are increasingly being detected in island water systems. These substances, while less well understood, pose long-term risks to both human and ecosystem health and highlight the need for updated monitoring and treatment approaches.

Addressing threats to water quality on small islands requires a combination of infrastructure investment, regulatory enforcement, public education, and adaptive management. By understanding and mitigating these threats, island communities can protect their most vital resource and safeguard public health and environmental sustainability.

6.2 Monitoring and Assessing Water Quality

Monitoring and assessing water quality are essential processes for ensuring the safety and reliability of water supplies on small islands. Given the heightened vulnerability to contamination and the limited alternatives if a primary source becomes compromised, regular and systematic assessment provides the information needed to protect public health, guide management decisions, and maintain community trust.

A comprehensive monitoring program begins with the identification of key water sources—including groundwater wells, rainwater tanks, surface water bodies, and desalinated supplies. Each source presents its own set of risks and should be monitored based on its particular vulnerabilities. For example, groundwater wells near the coast require frequent checks for salinity and microbial contamination, while rainwater tanks may be more susceptible to debris, roof runoff, or mosquito breeding.

Selecting appropriate parameters for testing is a crucial step in water quality monitoring. Common indicators include physical characteristics (such as color, turbidity, and odor), chemical constituents (including salinity, nitrates, and heavy metals), and biological parameters (such as coliform bacteria and other pathogens). The choice of parameters should reflect local conditions, sources of pollution, and potential health risks.

Regular sampling is necessary to detect trends, identify emerging problems, and provide early warning of contamination events. The frequency of sampling depends on the vulnerability of the source, the size of the user population, and regulatory requirements. Some sources, such as drinking water wells or community supplies, may require monthly or even weekly testing, while less frequently used sources might be monitored on a seasonal or annual basis.

The use of field testing kits, portable sensors, and laboratory analysis all contribute to effective monitoring. Field kits enable rapid on-site assessment of basic indicators, which is especially valuable in remote or resource-limited settings. More advanced laboratory testing may be needed for complex or low-concentration contaminants, requiring samples to be transported to regional facilities.

Data management and reporting are critical components of a monitoring program. Results should be recorded systematically, stored securely, and made accessible to relevant authorities and community leaders. Timely reporting of results, especially when issues are detected, enables rapid response to contamination events and ensures that the public receives accurate information and guidance.

Community involvement in water quality monitoring can greatly enhance program effectiveness. Training local volunteers or community health workers to collect samples, conduct simple tests, and report concerns builds local capacity and increases public awareness. Engaging the community also promotes transparency, fosters a sense of shared responsibility, and encourages adoption of safe water practices.

Effective monitoring and assessment support adaptive management by providing the evidence needed to evaluate interventions, identify priorities for investment, and adjust policies or practices as conditions change. By maintaining rigorous oversight of water quality, small islands can better protect their populations and ensure the sustainability of their precious water resources.

6.3 Water Treatment Solutions

Ensuring safe water for consumption and daily use requires appropriate treatment solutions, particularly on small islands where contamination risks are high and alternative sources may be limited. Effective water treatment protects public health, improves water quality, and supports overall resilience to environmental challenges. Selection of treatment options depends on the type of contaminants present, available resources, and the scale of supply, ranging from individual households to community systems.

Basic water treatment often begins with filtration. Physical filtration methods—such as sand filters, ceramic filters, or cloth screening—remove suspended solids, sediment, and some pathogens from water collected from rainwater tanks, surface sources, or shallow wells. These technologies are generally simple to operate, affordable, and well-suited to remote or resource-constrained island settings.

Disinfection is another essential component of water treatment. Chlorination is widely used due to its effectiveness in killing bacteria and viruses, as well as providing residual protection during storage and distribution. Chlorine tablets or liquid bleach can be used at the household level, while larger systems may rely on automatic dosing equipment. Alternatives include ultraviolet (UV) light systems, which disinfect water as it passes through a chamber exposed to UV radiation, and boiling, which is effective for small batches but less practical for larger volumes or routine use.

For islands facing issues with salinity, chemical contamination, or specific pollutants, more advanced treatment solutions may be necessary. Reverse osmosis units or other membrane filtration technologies can remove salts, heavy metals, and a wide range of dissolved contaminants, producing high-quality water suitable for drinking and cooking. While these systems are highly effective, they require a reliable energy supply, regular maintenance, and technical expertise, which can present challenges on remote islands.

Point-of-use treatment options provide flexibility for households or small groups. Portable filters, solar disinfection (using clear bottles left in sunlight), and chemical disinfectants offer practical means of improving water quality, especially in emergencies or where centralized systems are unavailable. Community education on the safe handling and storage of treated water is essential to prevent recontamination and maximize the health benefits of these solutions.

Centralized treatment plants may serve larger populations or key facilities, such as schools or health centers. These plants typically employ a combination of filtration, sedimentation, and disinfection processes. Regular monitoring, skilled operators, and ongoing maintenance are necessary to ensure consistent performance and protect against system failures.

Selecting appropriate water treatment solutions involves balancing effectiveness, cost, technical requirements, and community acceptance. Tailoring approaches to local conditions and ensuring adequate training and support helps sustain treatment systems over time. Investing in treatment capacity, both at the household and community level, strengthens water security and reduces vulnerability to waterborne diseases and environmental threats on small islands.

6.4 Safeguarding Watersheds and Recharge Areas

Protecting watersheds and recharge areas is fundamental to maintaining water quality and quantity on small islands. These natural systems capture, store, and filter rainfall, enabling the replenishment of groundwater and the sustainable functioning of surface water bodies. On islands where freshwater resources are limited and easily disrupted, safeguarding these areas is a key component of long-term water security and ecosystem health.

Watersheds are the land areas that drain rainwater into streams, rivers, or aquifers. On small islands, these zones are often small and can be highly sensitive to disturbance. Land use changes—such as deforestation, urbanization, or agricultural expansion—can reduce the ability of watersheds to absorb and filter water, leading to increased runoff, soil erosion, and pollution. Degraded watersheds lose their capacity to sustain clean water supplies, increase the risk of flooding, and diminish biodiversity.

Protecting natural vegetation within watersheds is one of the most effective strategies. Forests, wetlands, and native plant cover help slow down rainwater, promote infiltration into the ground, and trap sediments and contaminants before they reach water bodies. Reforestation or the restoration of degraded areas can significantly enhance these natural functions, supporting both water availability and quality.

Implementing land use planning and regulation helps control development activities that threaten recharge zones and watersheds. Zoning laws, conservation easements, and buffer zones around critical areas can limit construction, intensive agriculture, and other high-risk uses. Encouraging sustainable agricultural practices—such as minimizing chemical inputs, maintaining ground cover, and using contour planting—reduces the risk of nutrient runoff and pesticide pollution.

Community engagement is essential for the success of watershed protection. Local residents, farmers, and landowners play a direct role in managing and stewarding land, making their participation crucial in maintaining healthy recharge areas. Education campaigns, participatory mapping, and collaborative management agreements can foster a sense of ownership and responsibility while integrating traditional knowledge and practices.

Stormwater management is another important aspect. Installing green infrastructure—such as rain gardens, swales, and permeable pavements—enhances infiltration and reduces runoff in developed areas. These approaches not only protect recharge areas but also reduce the risk of flooding and downstream erosion.

Ongoing monitoring of watershed health is necessary to detect changes and guide management actions. Measuring indicators such as water levels, sediment loads, vegetation cover, and water quality helps track the effectiveness of protection measures and provides early warning of emerging problems.

Safeguarding watersheds and recharge areas on small islands requires a coordinated approach involving policy, science, and community action. By protecting these vital systems, island communities can secure their water future, enhance resilience to climate change, and support the broader integrity of their natural environment.

6.5 Community Engagement in Water Quality Protection

Community engagement is a vital component of water quality protection on small islands. Local residents, businesses, and organizations play a direct role in both the use and management of water resources, making their participation essential for the success of protection efforts. Involving the community fosters a sense of ownership, increases awareness of local challenges, and encourages the adoption of sustainable practices that safeguard water quality for all.

One effective approach to community engagement is education and outreach. Providing information about the sources of water contamination, safe water handling practices, and the importance of protecting catchment and recharge areas empowers people to make informed decisions. Schools, community centers, and local media can serve as platforms for sharing knowledge and promoting water-friendly behaviors, such as reducing litter, using environmentally safe products, and maintaining septic systems.

Participatory monitoring programs invite community members to help collect water samples, observe environmental changes, and report potential pollution sources. Training residents and local leaders in basic water quality testing builds local capacity and enables rapid identification of emerging problems. When community members are actively involved in monitoring, they are more likely to notice and respond to threats before they become serious.

Collaborative planning and decision-making ensure that local perspectives and traditional knowledge are integrated into water management strategies. Involving the community in setting priorities, developing protection plans, and designing interventions enhances relevance, legitimacy, and support for proposed actions. Community-led initiatives—such as clean-up days, tree planting, or watershed restoration—build momentum for water quality protection while strengthening social bonds.

Recognition and support for community champions—individuals or groups who advocate for water quality—can inspire broader participation and serve as examples for others to follow. Providing resources, training, or incentives to these leaders helps sustain engagement over the long term.

Community engagement is most effective when it is ongoing, inclusive, and adapted to the needs and culture of the island. By working together, island residents can create a strong foundation for water quality protection, ensuring safe and reliable water for present and future generations.

Chapter 7: Policy, Governance, and Institutional Frameworks

Robust policy, governance, and institutional frameworks are fundamental to achieving water security and resilience on small islands. Effective management of water resources requires clear policies, strong institutions, and inclusive governance structures that can coordinate across sectors and levels of government. This chapter examines the roles of national and local policies, the organization and capacity of institutions, and the importance of regulatory and financial frameworks in supporting sustainable water management and climate adaptation. Special attention is given to strengthening coordination, building technical and managerial capacity, and ensuring transparency, participation, and accountability. By aligning governance systems with the unique challenges and opportunities of island contexts, small islands can create enabling environments for long-term water security and adaptation success.

7.1 National and Local Policy Contexts

National and local policy frameworks form the foundation for effective water management on small islands. Policies and regulations shape how water resources are allocated, protected, and governed, influencing every aspect of supply, quality, and access. Given the unique vulnerabilities and constraints faced by small islands, developing clear, robust, and adaptive policy contexts is essential for achieving long-term water security and resilience.

At the national level, water policies typically set the overarching vision, objectives, and principles guiding the management of water resources. These policies may outline priorities such as universal access to safe water, protection of freshwater ecosystems, climate adaptation, and disaster risk reduction. National legislation provides the legal authority for managing water, establishing rights and responsibilities for users, and setting standards for water quality, allocation, and infrastructure development. On many small islands, water is recognized as a public good, and national policies aim to ensure equity, sustainability, and intergenerational fairness in its use.

Regulatory agencies or ministries are often mandated to oversee water management at the national scale. Their roles may include resource assessment, setting quality standards, licensing water abstraction, monitoring compliance, and coordinating responses to emergencies such as droughts or contamination events. Effective coordination between agencies—covering sectors such as environment, health, agriculture, and disaster management—is critical to addressing the complex and interrelated challenges of water management on islands.

Local policy contexts are equally important, as municipal governments, island councils, or community associations are typically responsible for day-to-day operations and maintenance of water systems. Local bylaws and regulations translate national policies into actionable measures, addressing issues such as water usage limits, tariff structures, land use controls, and waste management practices. These regulations are tailored to the specific needs and realities of each island or community, taking into account factors such as population size, available resources, infrastructure capacity, and traditional practices.

The alignment of national and local policies is crucial for effective water management. National frameworks should provide clear direction and resources, while allowing flexibility for local adaptation and innovation. Decentralization, where appropriate, can empower local authorities to manage water resources in ways that are responsive to local conditions and stakeholder input. However, this requires adequate technical, financial, and institutional support to ensure that local agencies can fulfill their mandates.

Policy integration is increasingly recognized as vital for managing water resources in a holistic way. Water policy should be coordinated with policies on land use, energy, waste, public health, and disaster preparedness, reflecting the interconnected nature of island systems. Integrated policy approaches help prevent conflicting objectives, promote synergies, and enable more efficient use of resources.

Inclusion and participation are essential elements of effective policy contexts. Developing and updating policies should involve consultation with communities, civil society, private sector actors, and other stakeholders. This ensures that diverse perspectives, traditional knowledge, and local priorities are reflected in policy decisions, increasing legitimacy and public support.

Finally, adaptive policy frameworks are needed to respond to the dynamic risks of climate change, population growth, and economic shifts. Regular review and revision of policies, informed by data and stakeholder feedback, ensure that water management remains relevant and effective in the face of emerging challenges.

By developing and maintaining strong national and local policy contexts, small islands can provide a solid foundation for water security, quality, and resilience, supporting sustainable development and the wellbeing of their communities.

7.2 Institutional Arrangements

Institutional arrangements are the structures and mechanisms through which water resources are managed, governed, and delivered on small islands. These arrangements determine who is responsible for planning, implementing, and overseeing water policies, as well as how different actors coordinate and collaborate. The effectiveness of institutional arrangements greatly influences the sustainability, equity, and resilience of water management systems.

On many small islands, water management responsibilities are distributed across several government departments or agencies. Ministries of environment, health, public works, and agriculture may each have roles related to water supply, quality monitoring, sanitation, and resource protection. While this division can leverage specialized expertise, it often leads to fragmented decision-making, overlapping mandates, and gaps in accountability. Clear delineation of responsibilities and effective coordination mechanisms are critical to overcoming these challenges.

Local government institutions—such as municipal councils, island authorities, or community water committees—often play a direct role in the operation and maintenance of water systems. These bodies may oversee distribution networks, collect user fees, organize repairs, and engage with residents about water issues. Their proximity to the community positions them to understand local needs and mobilize community participation. However, limited resources, technical capacity, or funding can constrain their effectiveness, particularly in responding to emergencies or implementing long-term improvements.

Water utilities or public service providers are frequently established to manage daily operations, including water treatment, distribution, and customer service. These entities may be publicly owned, private companies operating under contract, or community-managed organizations. The choice of utility model depends on local context, governance preferences, and the scale of water service delivery required.

Inter-institutional coordination is essential for managing water resources holistically. Formal mechanisms—such as interagency committees, joint task forces, or regular coordination meetings—can facilitate information sharing, joint planning, and the resolution of conflicts. Integrated water management is strengthened when institutions work together to align objectives, pool resources, and respond collectively to emerging challenges.

Non-governmental organizations, civil society groups, and the private sector also contribute to institutional arrangements by providing technical expertise, supporting capacity building, and implementing specific projects or initiatives. Their involvement can enhance innovation, mobilize resources, and expand the reach of water management programs.

Building strong institutional arrangements requires ongoing investment in human resources, training, and organizational development. Clear policies, transparent procedures, and accountability mechanisms underpin effective institutions. Regular review and adaptation of institutional frameworks are necessary to respond to changing conditions, such as population growth, climate impacts, or technological advances.

Robust institutional arrangements are foundational for achieving water security on small islands. By clarifying roles, promoting collaboration, and building capacity, islands can ensure that their water resources are managed efficiently, equitably, and sustainably for the benefit of all.

7.3 Financing Water Security and Adaptation (overview)

Financing is a cornerstone of achieving water security and enabling climate adaptation on small islands. Securing adequate and sustainable funding allows island communities to develop, maintain, and upgrade water infrastructure, implement resilience measures, and respond to emerging risks. However, small islands often face significant financial constraints due to limited revenue bases, small economies of scale, and high costs associated with importing materials, technology, or expertise.

Traditional sources of finance for water security typically include government budgets, user fees, and, in some cases, cross-subsidies between sectors. National governments may allocate funds for the construction and maintenance of water supply systems, wastewater treatment plants, and flood protection infrastructure. Local governments and utilities often rely on revenue from water tariffs to support daily operations and minor upgrades, though keeping tariffs affordable while ensuring financial sustainability can be a delicate balance.

External funding plays a crucial role for many small islands. International donors, development banks, and climate finance mechanisms provide grants, loans, or technical assistance for large capital projects, disaster recovery, or adaptation initiatives. Accessing such funds often requires meeting eligibility criteria, developing comprehensive proposals, and demonstrating capacity for implementation and reporting. Partnerships with regional organizations and neighboring islands can improve access to external finance and facilitate knowledge sharing.

Innovative financing mechanisms are gaining attention as islands seek to diversify funding sources and increase resilience. These include blended finance, green or blue bonds, and insurance schemes that transfer risk and provide resources for rapid recovery after disasters. Community-based financing, such as revolving funds or microfinance initiatives, can support local water projects and empower residents to invest in water security solutions.

To maximize the impact of available finance, small islands must strengthen financial management and planning capacities, ensure transparency in fund allocation, and prioritize investments that deliver long-term benefits. By leveraging a mix of funding sources and adopting innovative approaches, islands can better address water security and climate adaptation challenges while supporting sustainable development and community wellbeing.

7.4 Building Capacity and Technical Expertise

Building capacity and technical expertise is vital for the effective management of water resources and successful adaptation to climate change on small islands. Strengthening local skills, knowledge, and institutional capabilities enables island communities to plan, implement, and sustain water security measures in the face of ongoing challenges.

One of the first steps in building capacity is providing targeted training for water sector professionals, technicians, and utility staff. Training programs may cover topics such as water treatment, infrastructure maintenance, leak detection, water quality monitoring, and data management. Practical, hands-on learning ensures that personnel can operate and repair equipment, respond to emergencies, and troubleshoot common issues specific to island contexts. Building expertise in financial management, procurement, and regulatory compliance also supports effective utility operations and project delivery.

Education and awareness-raising for community members, local leaders, and schoolchildren expand the base of knowledge and foster a culture of water stewardship. Public workshops, school curricula, and community campaigns can help residents understand water challenges, the importance of conservation, and how to participate in protection efforts. Involving women, youth, and marginalized groups in capacity-building activities ensures that a broad cross-section of society contributes to and benefits from improved water management.

Institutional capacity development is equally important. Strengthening the ability of government agencies, local authorities, and community organizations to develop policies, coordinate activities, and manage resources underpins long-term resilience. This may involve organizational assessments, process improvements, information system upgrades, and the creation of multidisciplinary teams capable of addressing complex water and climate issues.

Regional and international partnerships provide valuable opportunities for capacity building. Collaborating with neighboring islands, universities, technical agencies, and development partners facilitates knowledge exchange, joint training, and access to specialized expertise. Participation in regional networks or professional associations keeps water professionals informed about new technologies, regulatory standards, and best practices.

Technical expertise in emerging areas—such as integrated water resources management, climate modeling, nature-based solutions, and innovative financing—enhances the ability of island communities to adopt new approaches and respond to changing risks. Training and recruiting specialists in these areas, or establishing advisory relationships with external experts, enables islands to remain at the forefront of water management innovation.

Sustaining capacity over time requires ongoing investment in human resources, knowledge sharing, and learning opportunities. Establishing mentorship programs, supporting continuing education, and creating incentives for staff retention all contribute to building a resilient and adaptable workforce.

By prioritizing capacity building and technical expertise, small islands can overcome many of the limitations posed by their size and isolation. Equipped with the right skills and knowledge, island communities are better prepared to secure their water future and adapt effectively to climate change.

7.5 Strengthening Inclusive and Adaptive Governance

Strengthening inclusive and adaptive governance is crucial for small islands striving to achieve water security and build resilience to climate change. Effective governance ensures that water resources are managed transparently, equitably, and flexibly, reflecting the needs and values of all segments of society while responding to evolving environmental and social pressures.

Inclusive governance starts with broadening participation in decision-making processes. Involving a wide range of stakeholders—including community members, women, youth, indigenous groups, local businesses, and civil society organizations—ensures that diverse perspectives, traditional knowledge, and local priorities are considered. Public consultations, advisory committees, and participatory planning workshops provide platforms for meaningful engagement, fostering ownership and trust in water management decisions. By addressing the needs of marginalized or vulnerable groups, inclusive governance helps to prevent inequities in water access and benefits.

Transparency and accountability are key elements of strong governance. Making information about water policies, plans, and system performance publicly available allows for informed dialogue and oversight. Mechanisms for grievance redress, reporting misconduct, and monitoring progress support accountability and help address conflicts or misunderstandings quickly and fairly. Transparent budgeting and financial reporting further enhance public confidence and support for water initiatives.

Adaptive governance emphasizes flexibility and learning in the face of uncertainty. Small islands face rapidly changing risks from climate variability, population shifts, and economic developments. Adaptive governance frameworks enable institutions to monitor conditions, assess emerging threats, and adjust strategies or regulations as new information becomes available. This approach relies on regular review of policies and plans, integrating lessons learned from past experiences and from other regions facing similar challenges.

Building the capacity of institutions and stakeholders to participate in adaptive governance is essential. Training in risk assessment, scenario planning, and monitoring and evaluation equips decision-makers with the tools needed to anticipate and manage change. Encouraging collaboration among agencies and sectors breaks down silos, promotes integrated solutions, and enhances the ability to respond to complex or cross-cutting challenges.

Promoting a culture of shared responsibility and stewardship is also important for long-term success. Encouraging active involvement in water management, recognizing community champions, and celebrating successful initiatives all help sustain engagement and motivation. Policy frameworks that reward innovation and learning, while maintaining clear standards and enforcement, support the continuous improvement of governance systems.

By strengthening inclusive and adaptive governance, small islands can better navigate the complexities of water management in a changing world. Such governance ensures that all voices are heard, decisions are transparent, and institutions remain responsive—laying the foundation for resilient, equitable, and sustainable water systems for generations to come.

Chapter 8: Community-Based Approaches and Social Resilience

Community-based approaches and social resilience are at the heart of effective water management and climate adaptation on small islands. The collective action, knowledge, and adaptive capacity of local communities are critical for safeguarding water resources, building preparedness for change, and responding quickly to emerging challenges. This chapter explores the diverse ways in which community participation, traditional practices, and local leadership contribute to water security. It highlights the importance of participatory planning, the integration of indigenous knowledge, and the building of social capital and adaptive capacity. By fostering a culture of resilience and empowering communities, small islands can develop tailored, inclusive solutions that are both practical and enduring, ensuring water security and well-being in the face of ongoing uncertainty.

8.1 The Role of Communities in Water Security

Communities play a central role in achieving water security on small islands. Given the close-knit nature of many island societies and the direct dependence of residents on local water sources, community engagement, leadership, and collective action are essential for the sustainable management and protection of water resources. Recognizing and empowering communities strengthens resilience, supports innovation, and ensures that solutions are tailored to the realities of island life.

Local communities are often the first to experience water scarcity, contamination, or infrastructure failures. Their immediate knowledge of environmental changes, social dynamics, and water use patterns provides valuable insights for identifying risks and designing effective responses. Community members can monitor local water sources, observe signs of pollution or overuse, and report issues more quickly than external authorities. This grassroots vigilance is particularly important on small islands where resources for centralized monitoring may be limited.

Communities also play a direct role in managing water supply systems, particularly in areas where government or utility reach is limited. In many cases, local water committees, cooperatives, or neighborhood associations organize the operation and maintenance of rainwater harvesting systems, wells, storage tanks, and distribution networks. Community-managed systems often benefit from a strong sense of ownership and accountability, resulting in better care, lower rates of vandalism or illegal connections, and faster response to technical problems.

Collective action extends to water conservation and demand management. When communities share a common understanding of the value and limitations of their water resources, they are more likely to adopt water-saving behaviors and support local regulations. Peer-to-peer education, public campaigns, and local champions can encourage habits such as fixing leaks, reducing waste, and reusing water. Involving schools, faith-based organizations, and youth groups helps embed conservation messages across generations and throughout society.

Traditional knowledge and cultural practices further enrich community roles in water security. Many island communities have developed indigenous water management systems—such as communal rainwater tanks, rotational water use, or customary protection of sacred springs—that have supported sustainable resource use for generations. Integrating this knowledge with scientific and technical approaches can enhance the effectiveness and acceptability of water security strategies.

Community participation is also vital in planning and policy-making. Including local voices in setting priorities, developing adaptation plans, and designing infrastructure ensures that interventions are responsive to actual needs and conditions. Participatory processes can reveal barriers to access, identify innovative solutions, and build consensus around difficult decisions, such as rationing during droughts or investing in new technologies.

Challenges exist, including disparities in access, capacity, and influence among different community groups. Efforts to promote equity and inclusion—ensuring the involvement of women, youth, marginalized groups, and those most affected by water challenges—are critical for fair and lasting outcomes. Capacity building through training, technical support, and financial assistance helps empower communities to take on leadership roles and manage increasingly complex systems.

By harnessing the collective power, local knowledge, and commitment of communities, small islands can build water security that is robust, adaptive, and resilient. Community engagement not only addresses immediate challenges but also lays the groundwork for sustainable water management in the face of climate change and other uncertainties.

8.2 Participatory Planning and Decision-Making

Participatory planning and decision-making are essential for effective and sustainable water management on small islands. Involving communities and stakeholders at every stage of the planning process ensures that water strategies reflect local realities, priorities, and knowledge, leading to greater ownership, legitimacy, and long-term success.

The participatory approach begins with open dialogue between authorities, water users, and affected groups. Early and ongoing consultations allow for the sharing of information, concerns, and ideas, helping to identify the specific water challenges faced by the community. This process uncovers insights that may be overlooked in top-down planning, such as seasonal shortages, traditional water use practices, or cultural preferences for certain sources.

Community workshops, public meetings, and focus groups are common methods for facilitating participation. These forums provide spaces for residents to voice their opinions, suggest solutions, and weigh the pros and cons of different options. Participatory mapping exercises can help communities identify water sources, vulnerable areas, and infrastructure gaps, while visioning sessions encourage residents to imagine desired future scenarios for water security.

Inclusion is a critical element of participatory planning. Special efforts should be made to involve women, youth, indigenous peoples, and marginalized groups, whose perspectives and needs may otherwise be underrepresented. Tailoring engagement methods to local languages and customs, as well as providing accessible meeting times and locations, increases the breadth and depth of participation.

Collaborative decision-making strengthens the effectiveness of water management interventions. By building consensus on priorities and solutions, communities are more likely to support and comply with new regulations, infrastructure investments, or behavior change campaigns. Transparent decision-making processes also help prevent conflicts and foster trust among stakeholders.

Feedback mechanisms, such as suggestion boxes, surveys, and regular progress updates, enable communities to continue contributing ideas and monitoring implementation. This ongoing engagement ensures that strategies remain relevant and that adjustments can be made as conditions change or new information becomes available.

Building the capacity of local leaders, facilitators, and organizations to lead participatory processes enhances the sustainability of these approaches. Training in facilitation, negotiation, and conflict resolution empowers communities to take an active role in shaping their water future.

Participatory planning and decision-making not only lead to better outcomes but also foster a sense of shared responsibility and collective action. By making community voices central to water management, small islands can develop solutions that are practical, inclusive, and resilient.

8.3 Traditional Knowledge and Practices

Traditional knowledge and practices play an important role in water management on small islands. Passed down through generations, these systems reflect a deep understanding of local environments, climate variability, and resource limitations. Integrating traditional approaches with modern science and technology can enhance the effectiveness, acceptance, and sustainability of water security strategies.

In many island communities, traditional water management revolves around the careful collection and use of rainwater. Communal tanks, stone cisterns, and shared wells have historically provided vital storage during dry seasons or droughts. The design, placement, and maintenance of these systems are often informed by generations of observation and experience, ensuring they are adapted to local rainfall patterns and community needs.

Customary rules and social norms guide water use and allocation. In some places, water resources are considered communal and governed by traditional leaders, elders, or councils. Systems of rotational access, seasonal restrictions, and sharing arrangements help distribute water equitably, reduce conflict, and prevent overuse. Sacred sites, such as springs or streams, may be protected from contamination or exploitation due to their cultural and spiritual significance.

Traditional practices also include methods for conserving and protecting water sources. Planting native trees around wells and recharge areas, using organic farming techniques, and maintaining vegetative buffers all help maintain water quality and encourage natural recharge. Indigenous techniques for soil and water conservation, such as terracing or mulching, support moisture retention and reduce runoff during heavy rains.

Storytelling, rituals, and community gatherings play a role in passing on water knowledge and reinforcing responsible behavior. Festivals that mark the start of the rainy season, ceremonies to bless water sources, or community clean-up days foster a sense of connection and stewardship, strengthening collective action for water security.

Adapting traditional knowledge to modern challenges requires collaboration and mutual respect between local communities, scientists, and policymakers. Joint research projects, participatory mapping, and the documentation of indigenous practices can help bridge the gap between customary and formal water management systems. Recognizing and protecting traditional water rights in legal frameworks ensures that customary users are included in decision-making and benefit from investments in infrastructure or adaptation.

There are challenges to sustaining traditional practices, including population growth, urbanization, and changing land use. Young people may be less familiar with traditional methods, and external pressures can erode communal management systems. Efforts to revitalize and integrate traditional knowledge should include education, intergenerational learning, and recognition of local leaders.

By valuing and incorporating traditional knowledge and practices, small islands can develop water management strategies that are culturally appropriate, locally accepted, and resilient. These approaches offer practical solutions for conservation, allocation, and stewardship, supporting both the well-being of communities and the sustainability of water resources.

8.4 Building Social Capital and Adaptive Capacity

Building social capital and adaptive capacity is essential for strengthening water security and climate resilience on small islands. Social capital refers to the networks of relationships, trust, and cooperation within a community, while adaptive capacity is the ability to anticipate, respond to, and recover from changing conditions and shocks. Together, these qualities empower communities to manage water resources more effectively and navigate uncertainty with confidence.

Social capital is developed through regular interaction, shared goals, and mutual support among community members. On small islands, where social ties are often strong and everyone depends on the same water sources, these networks facilitate the sharing of information, resources, and responsibilities. Community groups, water user associations, and informal support networks provide channels for collective action—organizing maintenance, responding to emergencies, and advocating for improvements in water management. Trust among residents increases the likelihood of compliance with conservation measures, reporting of leaks or pollution, and acceptance of necessary restrictions during droughts.

Adaptive capacity builds on social capital by enabling communities to anticipate future risks, plan for diverse scenarios, and adjust to changing circumstances. On small islands, this may involve developing early warning systems for storms or droughts, diversifying water sources to reduce dependence on a single supply, and encouraging the use of innovative technologies or practices. Communities with high adaptive capacity are better prepared to absorb shocks—such as infrastructure failures, contamination events, or extreme weather—and recover more quickly when they occur.

Leadership and inclusive participation are key components of both social capital and adaptive capacity. Strong local leadership helps mobilize resources, coordinate activities, and communicate priorities within and beyond the community. Ensuring that women, youth, and marginalized groups are included in decision-making processes strengthens social cohesion and broadens the range of skills and knowledge available to address challenges.

Capacity building supports both social capital and adaptive capacity. Training programs, peer-to-peer learning, and knowledge exchange with other islands or regions enhance the skills and understanding of community members and leaders. Encouraging communities to engage in monitoring, evaluation, and learning from past experiences fosters a culture of reflection and continuous improvement.

External partnerships can reinforce local efforts. Collaborating with government agencies, non-governmental organizations, and regional networks brings additional expertise, technical support, and financial resources. Such partnerships can introduce new tools, share best practices, and help communities access funding for resilience-building activities.

Maintaining and nurturing social capital and adaptive capacity is an ongoing process. Regular community meetings, joint problem-solving activities, and recognition of contributions all help sustain engagement and motivation. By investing in these social foundations, small islands can enhance their resilience to climate and water challenges, ensure the sustainability of their water systems, and build stronger, more united communities.

8.5 Fostering a Culture of Resilience

Fostering a culture of resilience is vital for small islands aiming to secure their water future and adapt to ongoing environmental and social changes. A resilient culture is one in which individuals, households, and communities proactively prepare for, respond to, and recover from disruptions—whether these are caused by climate variability, extreme weather events, or resource shortages.

Creating this culture begins with raising awareness of risks and building shared understanding of the importance of preparedness and adaptation. Education campaigns in schools, public forums, and community meetings can highlight local vulnerabilities and the practical steps everyone can take to strengthen resilience. Storytelling, the sharing of past experiences, and celebrating successful responses to challenges reinforce the message that resilience is both possible and necessary.

Encouraging community participation in planning and decision-making builds a sense of ownership and responsibility. When residents help design water management strategies, participate in drills or emergency planning, and contribute to monitoring efforts, they become invested in both the process and the outcome. This shared engagement increases readiness and willingness to act quickly when threats arise.

Recognition and support for local champions—individuals or groups who advocate for resilience, lead initiatives, or support their neighbors—help spread best practices and motivate others. Incentives such as awards, public acknowledgment, or small grants for community-led projects can sustain momentum and broaden participation.

Regular reflection and learning from experience also help embed resilience as a core value. After major events or near-misses, communities can come together to assess what worked, what didn't, and how to improve for the future. This adaptive mindset ensures that resilience is not a one-time effort but an ongoing part of community life.

By fostering a culture of resilience, small islands equip themselves to face uncertainty with confidence and cooperation, ensuring that water security and well-being are preserved for future generations.

Chapter 9: Financing Water Security and Adaptation in Small Islands

Securing adequate and sustainable financing is a major challenge for small islands striving to achieve water security and climate resilience. The high costs of infrastructure, limited local revenue, and vulnerability to climate impacts demand innovative and diversified approaches to finance. This chapter examines the specific financial constraints facing small islands, reviews the range of funding sources available—including public budgets, donor assistance, climate finance, and private investment—and explores strategies for mobilizing and managing these resources effectively. Key topics include the importance of building financial sustainability, strengthening governance and capacity, and leveraging partnerships to unlock new funding opportunities. By addressing the financing challenge, small islands can develop and maintain the robust water systems and adaptive capacities necessary to support sustainable development and protect communities from the growing risks of climate change.

9.1 The Financing Challenge for Small Islands

Financing water security and adaptation initiatives poses a significant challenge for small islands. These territories often face a complex mix of constraints that make it difficult to generate, access, and sustain the funds needed to address water scarcity, infrastructure needs, and the escalating risks associated with climate change. Understanding the nature of these financial challenges is crucial for developing strategies that can support resilient water management.

One of the most pressing issues is the limited fiscal capacity of small island governments. With small economies, narrow tax bases, and high dependence on sectors like tourism or agriculture, many islands have constrained public budgets. This limits the ability of local authorities to fund new infrastructure projects, maintain aging water systems, or invest in advanced technologies for treatment, monitoring, or conservation. High import costs for materials and equipment—driven by geographic isolation—increase the overall price tag for infrastructure upgrades and repairs.

Another challenge is the lack of economies of scale. Small populations mean that the cost per capita for large projects is significantly higher than in larger countries, making investments in water supply, wastewater treatment, or desalination more expensive to deliver and operate. Small islands often struggle to attract private investment, as limited markets and higher perceived risks can deter commercial financiers and technology providers.

Access to external finance is critical but comes with its own hurdles. While international donors, development banks, and climate funds offer grants, loans, and technical assistance, competition for these resources is intense, and the application processes are often complex and resource-intensive. Meeting eligibility criteria and preparing strong proposals require skills and institutional capacity that may be lacking at the local level. Once funding is secured, reporting and compliance requirements can further strain limited administrative resources.

Uncertainty and risk related to climate change make financial planning even more complicated. Frequent storms, droughts, or sea level rise can cause sudden and severe damage to infrastructure, disrupting services and creating unexpected costs. The need for both preventive investments and post-disaster recovery funding adds to the burden on already stretched budgets. Insurance and risk transfer mechanisms are often underutilized due to lack of awareness, affordability concerns, or the absence of tailored products for island contexts.

Balancing affordability with cost recovery is a persistent issue. Setting water tariffs high enough to support operation and maintenance, while keeping them affordable for households and businesses, can be challenging—especially where poverty rates are high or incomes are seasonal and uncertain.

Addressing the financing challenge requires a multifaceted approach. Strengthening domestic resource mobilization, building capacity to access and manage external funds, and leveraging innovative finance mechanisms—such as blended finance, green bonds, or revolving funds—can all contribute to greater financial sustainability. Partnerships with regional organizations and the private sector may also help unlock new resources and share risks.

By recognizing and strategically addressing these financial challenges, small islands can improve their prospects for securing the funding needed to build and maintain resilient water systems, adapt to climate impacts, and support sustainable development.

9.2 Sources of Finance

Securing a diverse mix of funding sources is essential for small islands aiming to achieve water security and climate adaptation. Relying on a single source is rarely sufficient or sustainable, particularly given the scale of investment needed and the vulnerability of island economies to shocks. By understanding and leveraging a range of financial options, small islands can strengthen their capacity to deliver critical water projects and build long-term resilience.

1. Public Sector Funding:

The primary source of finance for water infrastructure and adaptation projects on most small islands is public funding from national and local governments. Government budgets may allocate resources for capital investments, maintenance, and emergency response. In many cases, water utilities or municipal authorities also generate revenue through user fees or tariffs, which help cover operational expenses. However, limited fiscal capacity and competing priorities can constrain the size and reliability of public funding.

2. International Development Assistance:

Development aid from bilateral and multilateral donors remains a significant source of finance for small island states. International organizations—such as the World Bank, Asian Development Bank, Caribbean Development Bank, European Union, and United Nations agencies—provide grants, concessional loans, and technical assistance for water supply, wastewater treatment, disaster risk reduction, and climate adaptation. Bilateral aid from countries with longstanding relationships or regional interests also supports infrastructure upgrades, capacity building, and policy reform. Accessing these funds often requires strong project proposals, institutional capacity for implementation, and compliance with donor requirements.

3. Climate Finance Mechanisms:

Specialized climate finance instruments have become increasingly important for funding adaptation and resilience-building on small islands. The Green Climate Fund (GCF), Adaptation Fund, Global Environment Facility (GEF), and other climate-focused funds offer resources for projects that address climate risks, protect water resources, and reduce greenhouse gas emissions. These mechanisms are particularly relevant for islands facing acute climate impacts, but the application process is competitive and often requires technical expertise.

4. Private Sector Investment:

While less common, private investment is a potential source of finance for water security projects, particularly when there are opportunities for cost recovery or revenue generation. Public-private partnerships (PPPs), build-operate-transfer (BOT) schemes, and concessions can attract private capital and technical expertise for the development, operation, or management of water infrastructure. Innovative business models—such as water vending, decentralized treatment systems, or renewable energy-powered desalination—may appeal to private investors where market conditions are favorable. Creating an enabling environment with clear regulations, risk-sharing mechanisms, and transparent procurement processes is essential for attracting private finance.

5. Community-Based and Local Financing:

Community savings groups, cooperatives, and microfinance institutions can play a valuable role in funding small-scale water projects. Local financing mechanisms, such as revolving funds or community water trusts, support investments in rainwater harvesting, household connections, or small treatment systems. These approaches foster ownership, build local capacity, and help bridge funding gaps for projects that may be too small or context-specific for larger donors or investors.

6. Innovative and Blended Finance:

Blended finance approaches combine public, private, and donor resources to mobilize larger volumes of capital for water security and adaptation. Instruments such as green bonds, blue bonds, resilience bonds, and insurance products are increasingly being tailored to small island needs. For example, catastrophe bonds can provide rapid payouts after extreme events, while insurance pools spread risk across multiple countries or sectors. Results-based finance—where disbursement is linked to the achievement of specific outcomes—can incentivize efficient and impactful project delivery.

7. Regional and Multilateral Mechanisms:

Regional development banks, intergovernmental organizations, and regional trust funds offer tailored support to groups of islands facing similar challenges. Pooling resources, sharing technical assistance, and developing joint projects enhance access to finance and promote knowledge exchange across the region.

By drawing on this wide spectrum of finance sources, small islands can build resilient water systems, adapt to a changing climate, and support the wellbeing and prosperity of their communities. Developing strong financial management, project preparation, and partnership-building skills is essential for unlocking and effectively utilizing these diverse funding streams.

9.3 Mobilizing Private Sector Investment

Mobilizing private sector investment is increasingly recognized as a critical strategy for addressing water security and adaptation needs on small islands. While public funds and donor assistance remain important, the scale of investment required to modernize infrastructure, introduce innovative technologies, and build climate resilience often exceeds the capacity of governments and development agencies alone. Engaging the private sector can unlock new capital, bring technical expertise, and foster innovation, helping to fill critical financing gaps.

One pathway for attracting private investment is through public-private partnerships (PPPs). In these arrangements, governments and private companies collaborate to finance, build, operate, or maintain water infrastructure. PPPs can take a variety of forms, such as build-operate-transfer (BOT) contracts, management concessions, or service agreements. These models allow governments to share risks and costs while benefiting from private sector efficiency and technical know-how. Clear legal frameworks, transparent procurement processes, and fair risk-sharing are essential for attracting and sustaining private interest.

Creating an enabling environment for private investment is equally important. Small islands must establish and enforce policies and regulations that provide clarity, stability, and confidence to investors. This includes ensuring transparent tariff-setting, honoring contractual obligations, and upholding property and investment rights. Regulatory bodies can also play a role in monitoring service quality, setting performance standards, and resolving disputes, building trust among all stakeholders.

Innovative business models offer new opportunities for private sector engagement. Small-scale water enterprises, decentralized treatment solutions, and renewable energy-powered desalination plants are examples of investments that can generate returns while delivering social and environmental benefits. Digital technologies—such as smart metering, leak detection, and mobile payment systems—present additional avenues for investment, particularly in islands with growing tourism or urban populations.

Blended finance approaches, which combine public, donor, and private funds, can help reduce risk and improve the attractiveness of water projects. Guarantees, grants, concessional loans, and insurance mechanisms may be used to mitigate financial and political risks for private investors, making it more feasible to invest in challenging island contexts. International climate funds and development finance institutions increasingly offer tools designed to leverage private capital in support of resilience and adaptation goals.

Capacity building for both the public and private sectors is vital. Governments and local authorities must be able to design, negotiate, and manage complex contracts, while private firms need to understand the unique risks, opportunities, and social dynamics of small islands. Partnerships with regional business associations, technical advisors, and multilateral agencies can provide training, technical assistance, and market intelligence to support successful investment.

By mobilizing private sector investment, small islands can access new financial resources, introduce cutting-edge technologies, and accelerate progress toward water security and climate resilience. Effective collaboration, clear governance, and a focus on mutual benefits are key to creating lasting partnerships that deliver value for both investors and island communities.

9.4 Building Financial Sustainability

Building financial sustainability is a cornerstone of long-term water security and climate resilience for small islands. Financial sustainability ensures that water services and adaptation measures are not only initiated but can also be maintained, upgraded, and scaled over time without constant dependence on unpredictable external grants or emergency funds. Achieving this requires a careful balance between affordability for users, cost recovery for utilities, and effective use of available financial resources.

A key element of financial sustainability is the design of tariff structures and revenue systems that reflect the true cost of service delivery. Transparent and equitable pricing allows for adequate cost recovery while ensuring that essential water services remain accessible to all, including vulnerable and low-income households. Tiered tariffs, lifeline rates for basic consumption, and targeted subsidies can help balance social equity with the need for financial viability. Regular reviews and adjustments of tariffs, based on updated cost and demand data, are necessary to keep pace with inflation, operational changes, and investment needs.

Operational efficiency also underpins financial sustainability. Reducing water losses through leak detection, regular maintenance, and efficient billing systems helps maximize available resources and minimize unnecessary expenditures. Investments in smart technology—such as automated metering, remote monitoring, and digital payment platforms—can streamline operations, reduce costs, and improve revenue collection. Building local capacity for maintenance and repairs minimizes costly downtime and dependence on external technical support.

Diversifying funding sources is crucial to reduce vulnerability to shocks and changing funding landscapes. While user fees and government transfers remain important, small islands can explore additional revenue streams such as public-private partnerships, innovative financing mechanisms, or community-based funds.

Establishing reserve funds or contingency accounts provides a buffer for unanticipated expenses, emergencies, or future capital investments.

Financial planning and management are essential components of sustainability. Utilities and water authorities should develop long-term financial plans that account for operating costs, capital investments, debt servicing, and future growth. Transparent budgeting, regular financial reporting, and independent audits foster accountability and help build trust among stakeholders, including the public, investors, and donors.

Capacity building in financial management is equally important. Training for utility managers, local officials, and community leaders in budgeting, accounting, procurement, and reporting strengthens the overall financial health of water systems. Engaging stakeholders in financial decision-making—such as through advisory boards or public consultations—ensures that priorities are aligned and that trade-offs are understood and accepted.

By focusing on financial sustainability, small islands can safeguard their water infrastructure, maintain service quality, and ensure that communities remain resilient in the face of changing climate and economic conditions. Proactive financial strategies provide the foundation for reliable water services and long-term adaptation, supporting the well-being and prosperity of island residents.

9.5 Strengthening Financial Governance and Capacity

Strengthening financial governance and capacity is essential for small islands to achieve lasting water security and effective climate adaptation. Sound financial governance ensures that funds are managed transparently, efficiently, and in alignment with local priorities, while strong financial capacity enables the planning, implementation, and monitoring of projects that address both current needs and future risks.

A core component of financial governance is the establishment of clear policies and procedures for budgeting, procurement, expenditure, and reporting. Transparent rules and regular audits reduce the risk of mismanagement, corruption, or inefficiency. By adhering to recognized standards and involving independent oversight—such as audit committees or external reviewers—water authorities and local governments build public trust and credibility with donors, investors, and the community.

Capacity building in financial management is equally important. Training staff in budgeting, accounting, project appraisal, and fund management enhances the ability of institutions to make sound financial decisions and adapt to changing conditions. Developing skills in preparing funding proposals, managing grant agreements, and meeting donor reporting requirements increases access to external resources and improves compliance with funding conditions.

Strong coordination between agencies and levels of government supports better financial planning and resource allocation. Integrated financial management systems, regular inter-agency meetings, and shared databases allow for efficient tracking of expenditures and alignment of budgets with strategic objectives. Clear communication channels and joint planning also minimize duplication and make it easier to respond to emergencies or shifting priorities.

Promoting financial literacy and engagement among stakeholders is another key aspect of financial governance. Involving community representatives, user groups, and local leaders in budget reviews, tariff-setting, or investment planning increases transparency and accountability. Public consultations and regular updates on financial performance foster ownership and support for cost recovery or new investments.

Strengthening financial governance and capacity provides small islands with the tools to manage their water resources more sustainably, attract new funding, and deliver lasting benefits for their communities. By embedding good financial practices throughout water management systems, islands are better positioned to meet the challenges of climate change and development with confidence and resilience.

Conclusion

Small islands face a unique convergence of challenges in securing water resources and adapting to climate change. The constraints of geography, limited freshwater sources, and increasing climatic risks require holistic and context-specific strategies. Throughout this book, we have explored the vulnerability of small islands, the range of water sources and management tools available, and the crucial roles played by governance, finance, infrastructure, and community action. The experiences and lessons of small islands illustrate that resilience is not only a technical challenge, but also a social, economic, and institutional one—demanding coordinated action at all levels. By understanding and addressing these interlinked dimensions, small islands can protect their most precious resource and chart a path toward a sustainable and secure future.

Summarizing Key Messages

Water security and climate resilience for small islands depend on integrated management, diversification of sources, and protection of natural recharge areas. Building adaptive infrastructure, promoting demand management, and protecting water quality are vital elements of a robust response. Governance and policy frameworks must be inclusive, adaptive, and capable of aligning national priorities with local realities. Finance is both a barrier and an opportunity, making it essential to develop a blend of funding sources—public, private, and external—while focusing on financial sustainability and transparent management. The participation and empowerment of communities stand at the heart of effective water management, with traditional knowledge, collective action, and local stewardship providing a foundation for enduring resilience. By strengthening these pillars, small islands can respond proactively to current pressures and future uncertainties.

Moving Forward

Looking ahead, small islands must continue to innovate and adapt. This involves investing in nature-based and technological solutions, enhancing data collection and monitoring, and building capacity at every level—from community groups to government agencies. Collaboration across sectors, regions, and international partners will be critical in accessing knowledge, finance, and technical support. Maintaining flexibility and openness to new ideas allows small islands to adjust strategies as circumstances change, ensuring that policies and investments remain relevant and effective. Strengthening the links between policy, practice, and community needs will help maintain momentum and build the public trust necessary for bold adaptation measures.

A Call to Action

The urgency of water security and climate resilience for small islands cannot be overstated. Decision-makers, practitioners, and communities must seize the opportunity to act now, before further crises emerge. Investing in water infrastructure, advancing inclusive governance, and building financial capacity are all essential steps. At the same time, fostering a culture of resilience—where learning, adaptation, and shared responsibility are valued—will equip small islands to thrive despite uncertainty. Every individual, from government leaders to residents, has a role to play. By working together and making water security a priority, small islands can transform vulnerability into resilience and ensure a safe, prosperous future for generations to come.

www.ingramcontent.com/pod-product-compliance
Lightning Source LLC
Chambersburg PA
CBHW070644240926
51846CB00003BA/780
9781991370914